Dtp
and
graphic design

Iacob Adrian

Dante's Inferno Illustrations

vol. 1

Iacob Adrian

ISBN-13 : 978-1479340255
ISBN-10 : 1479340251

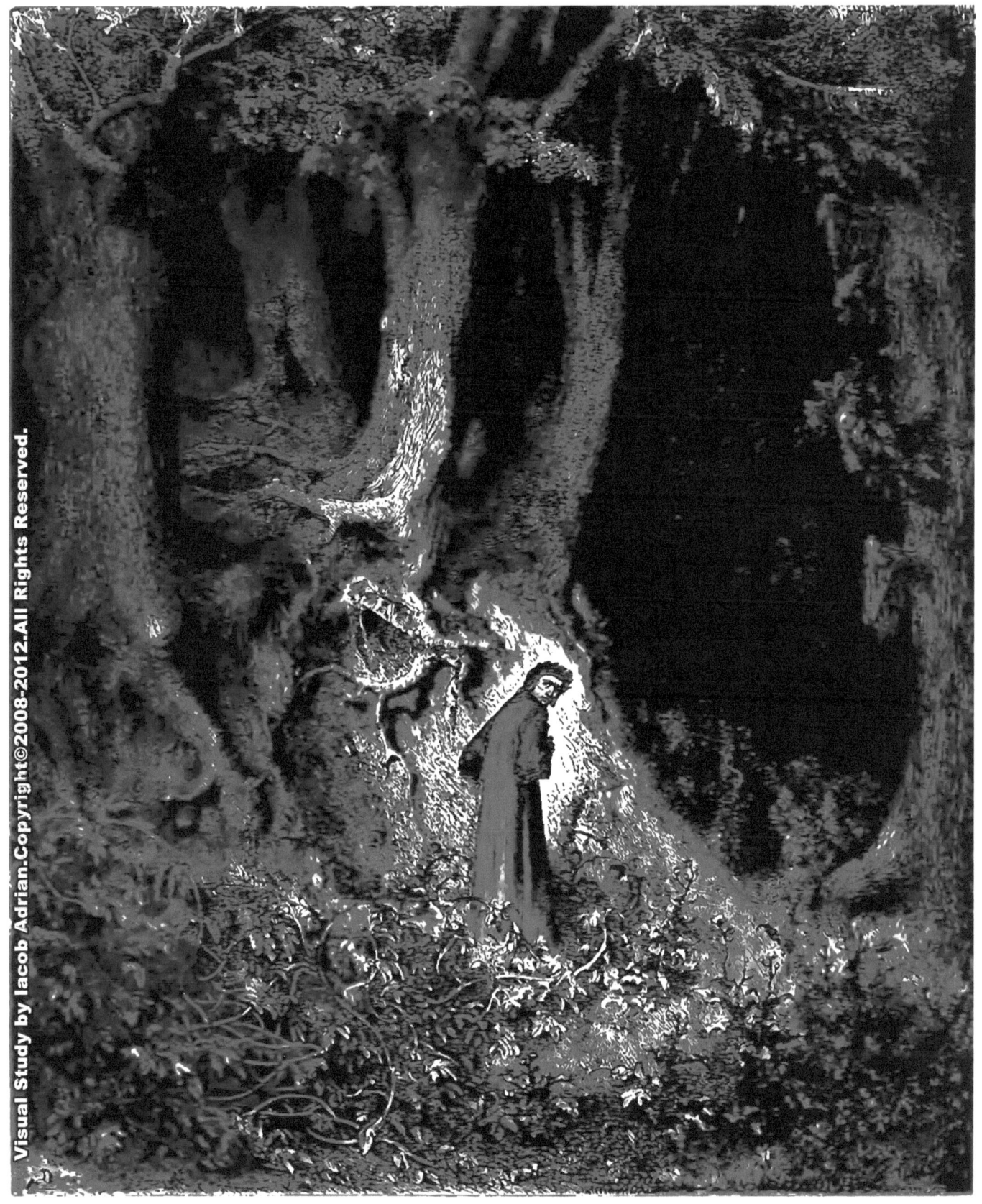

In the midway of this our mortal life,
I found me in a gloomy wood, astray.

Canto I., lines 1. 2.

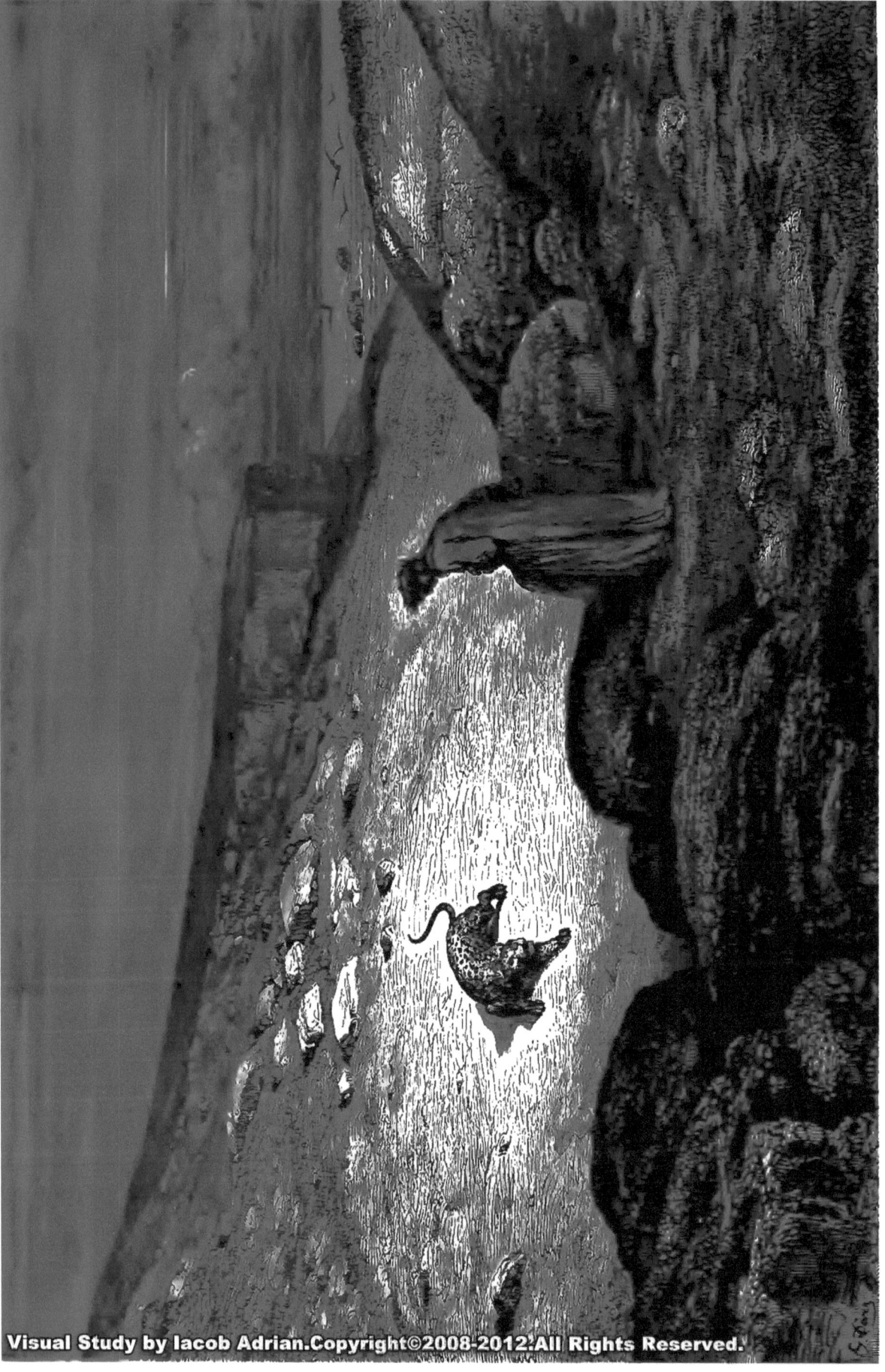

Scarce the ascent
Began, when, lo! a panther, nimble, light,
And cover'd with a speckled skin, appear'd;
Nor, when it saw me, vanish'd.
Canto I., lines 29—32.

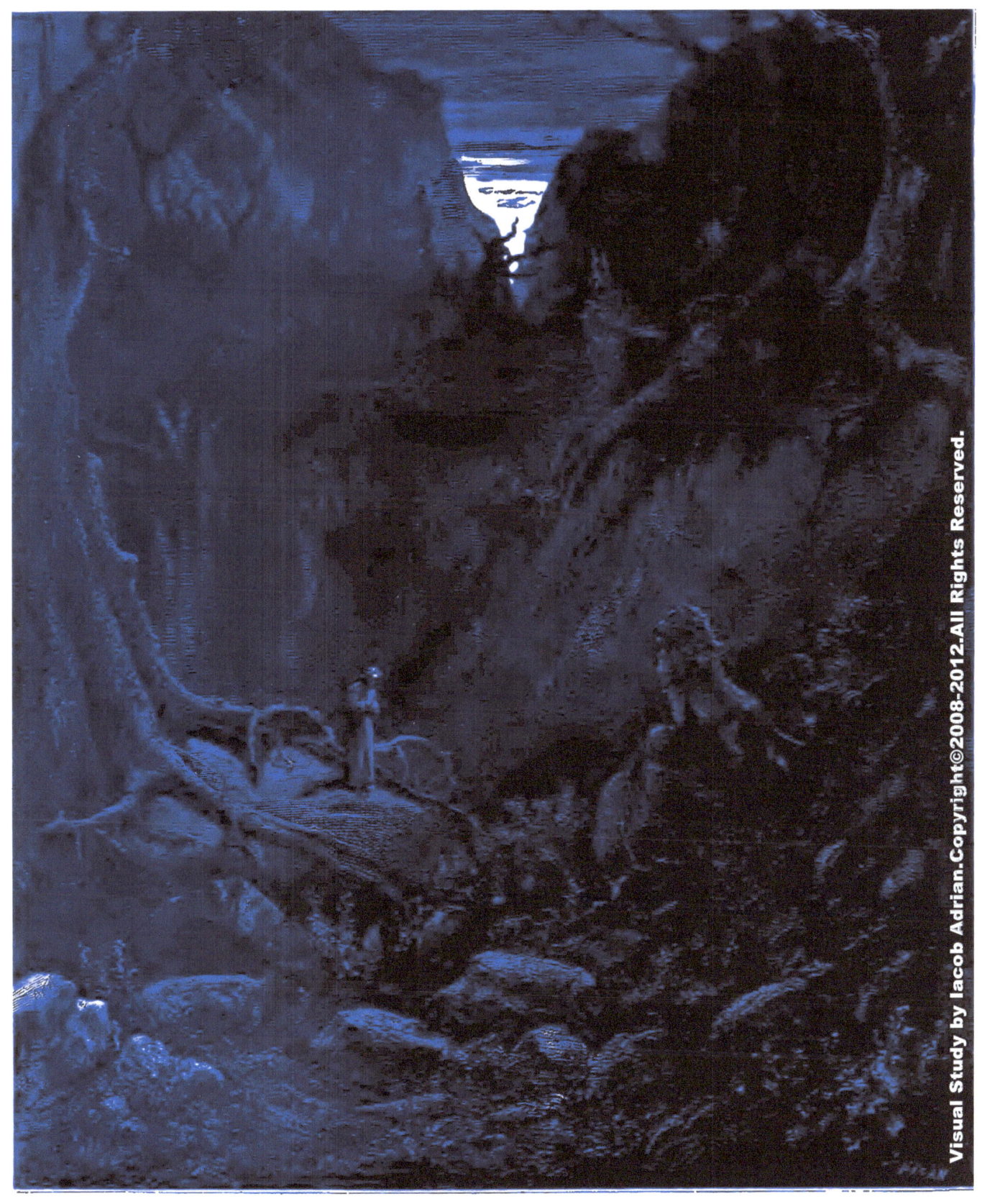

A lion came, 'gainst me as it appear'd,
With his head held aloft, and hunger-mad.

Canto I., lines 43, 44.

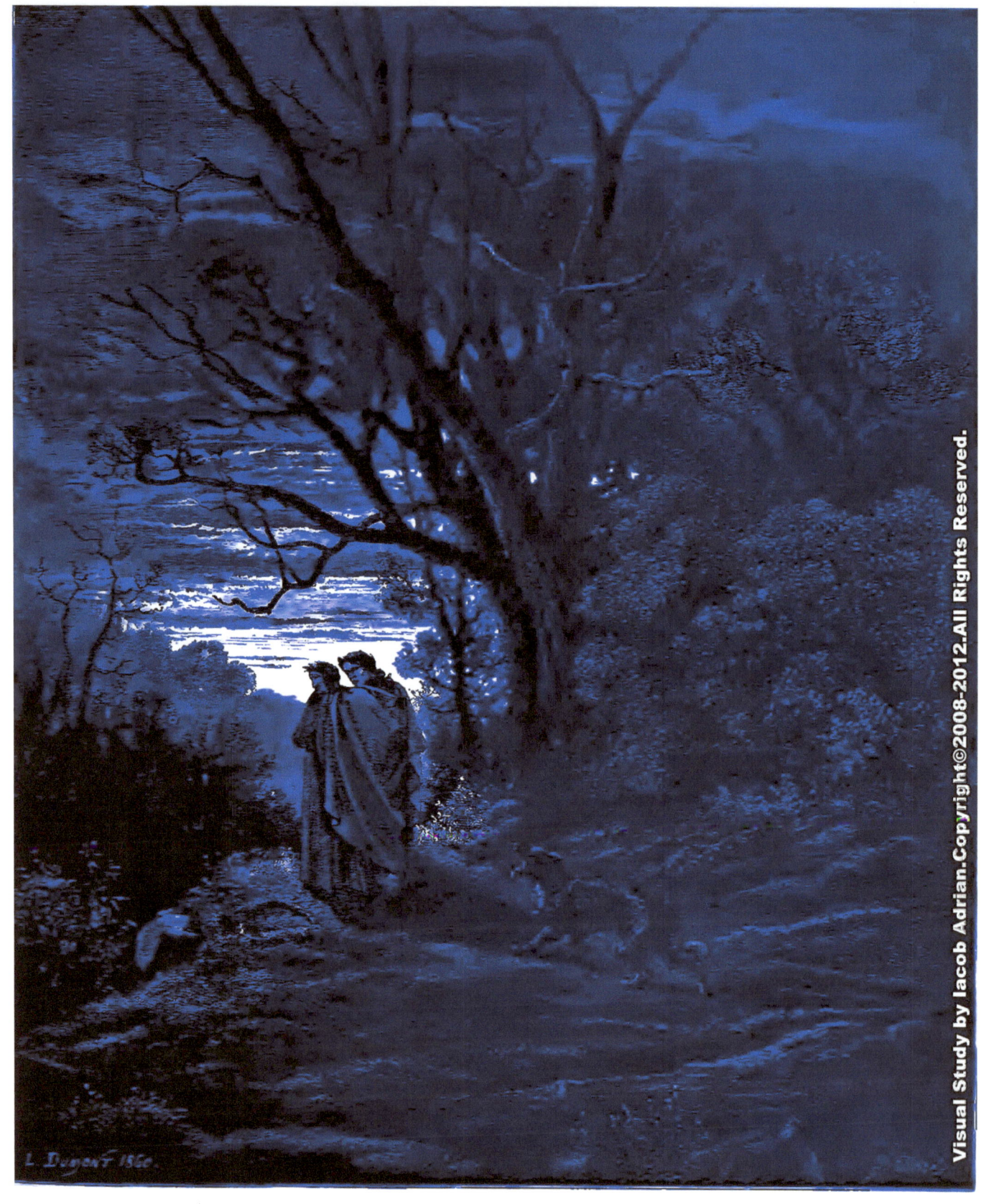

He soon as he saw
That I was weeping, answer'd.

Canto I., lines 87, 88.

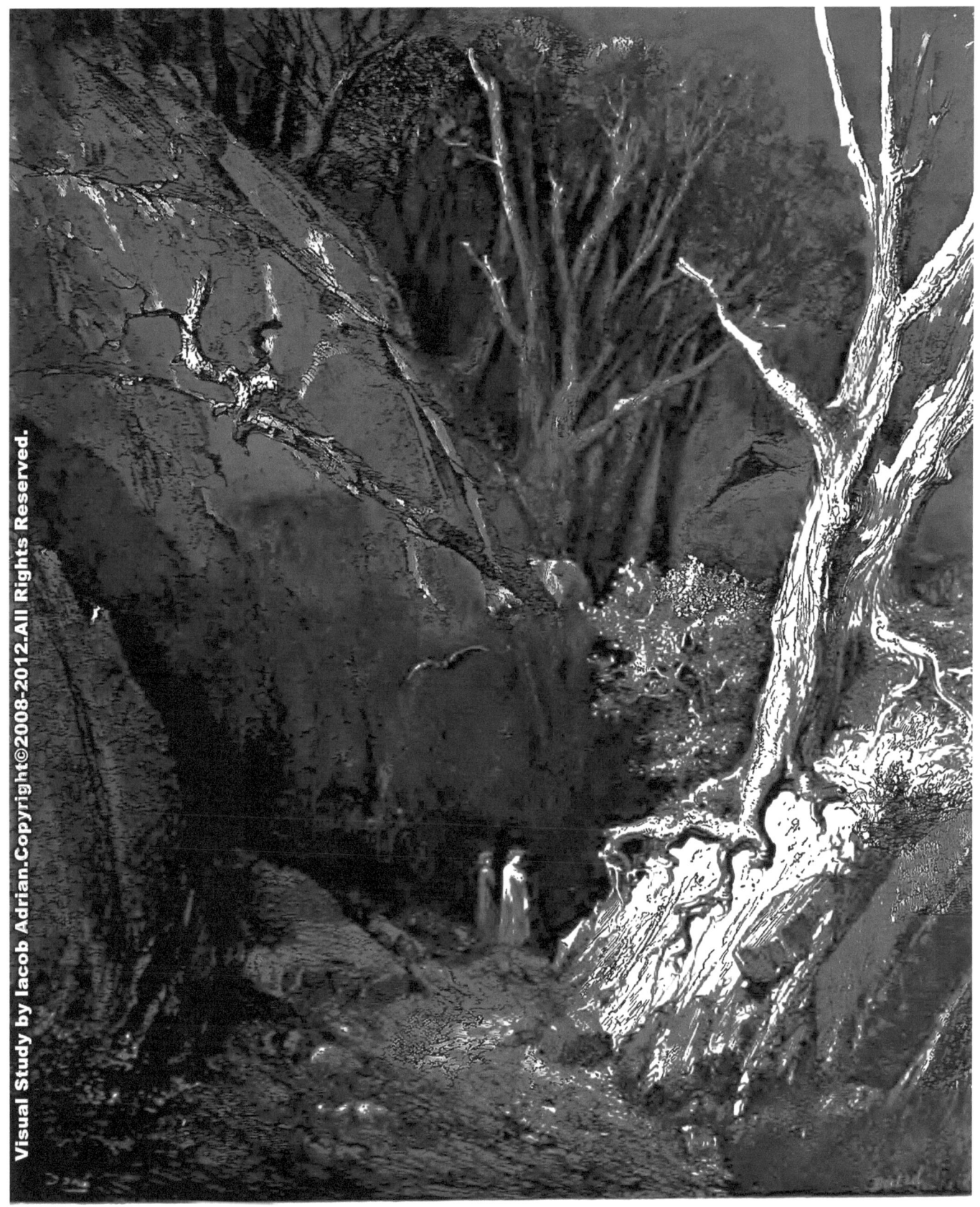

Onward he moved, I close his steps pursued.

Canto I., line 132.

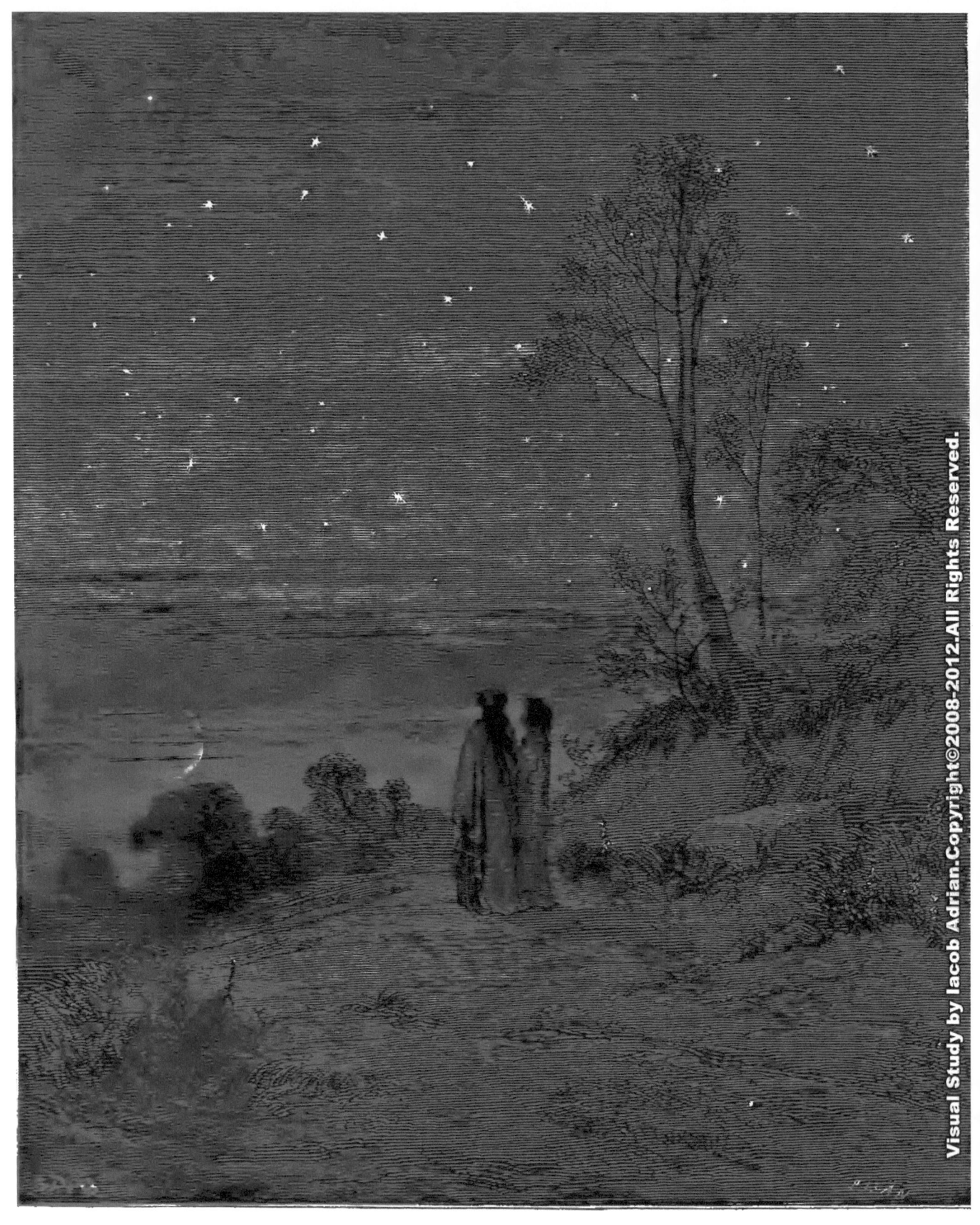

Now was the day departing.

Canto II., line 1.

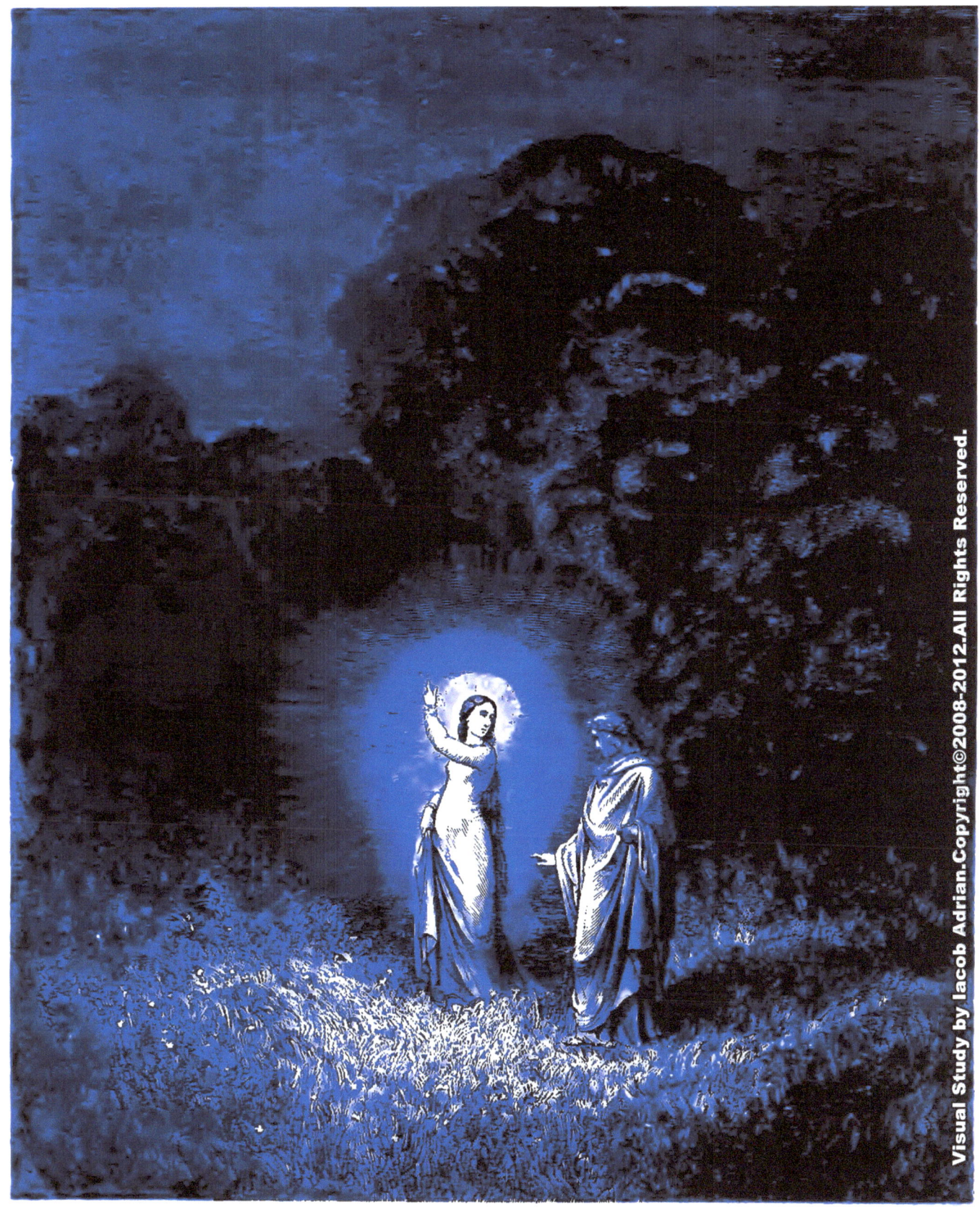

I, who now bid thee on this errand forth,
Am Beatrice.

Canto II., lines 70, 71.

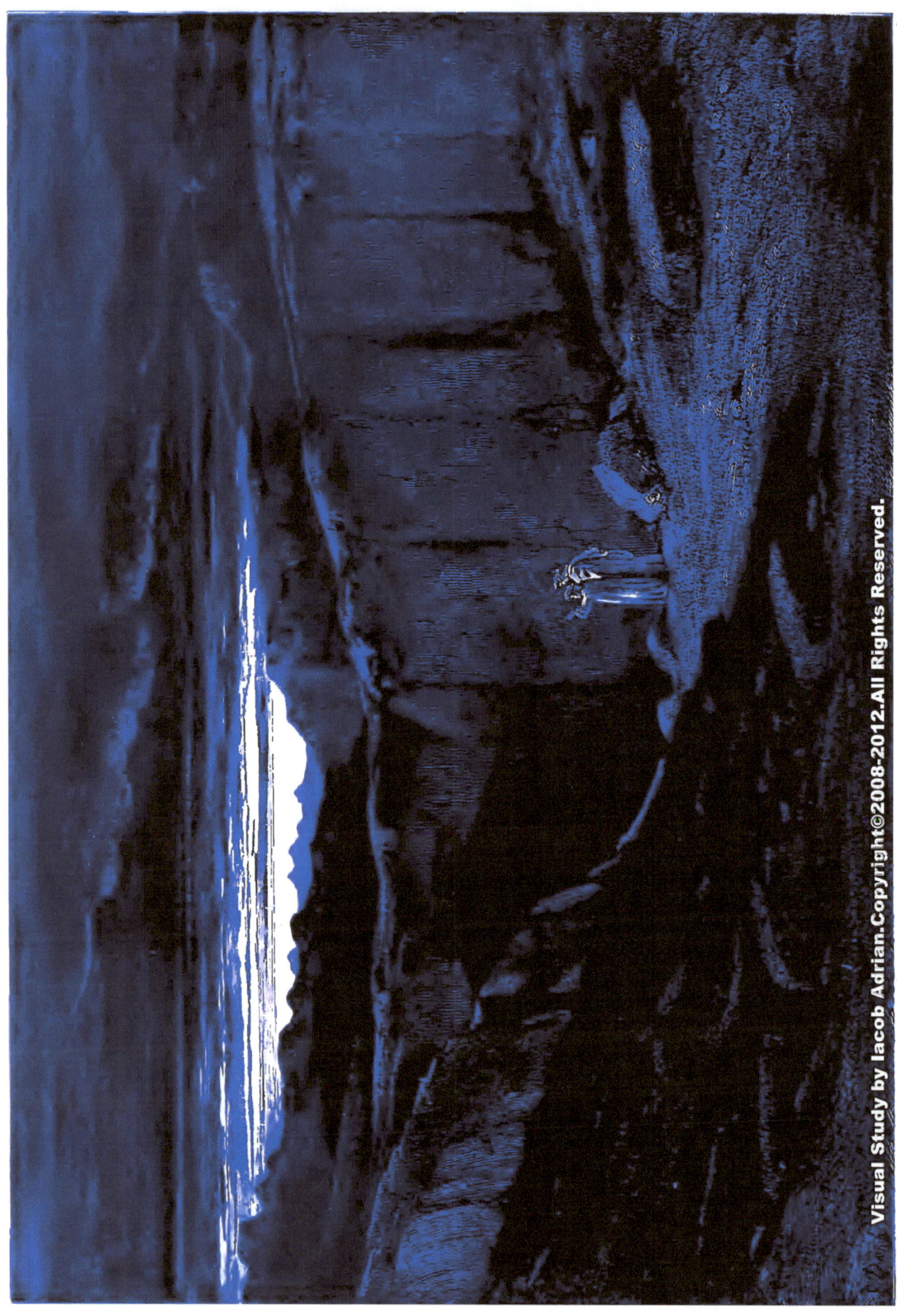

All hope abandon, ye who enter here.
Canto III., line 9.

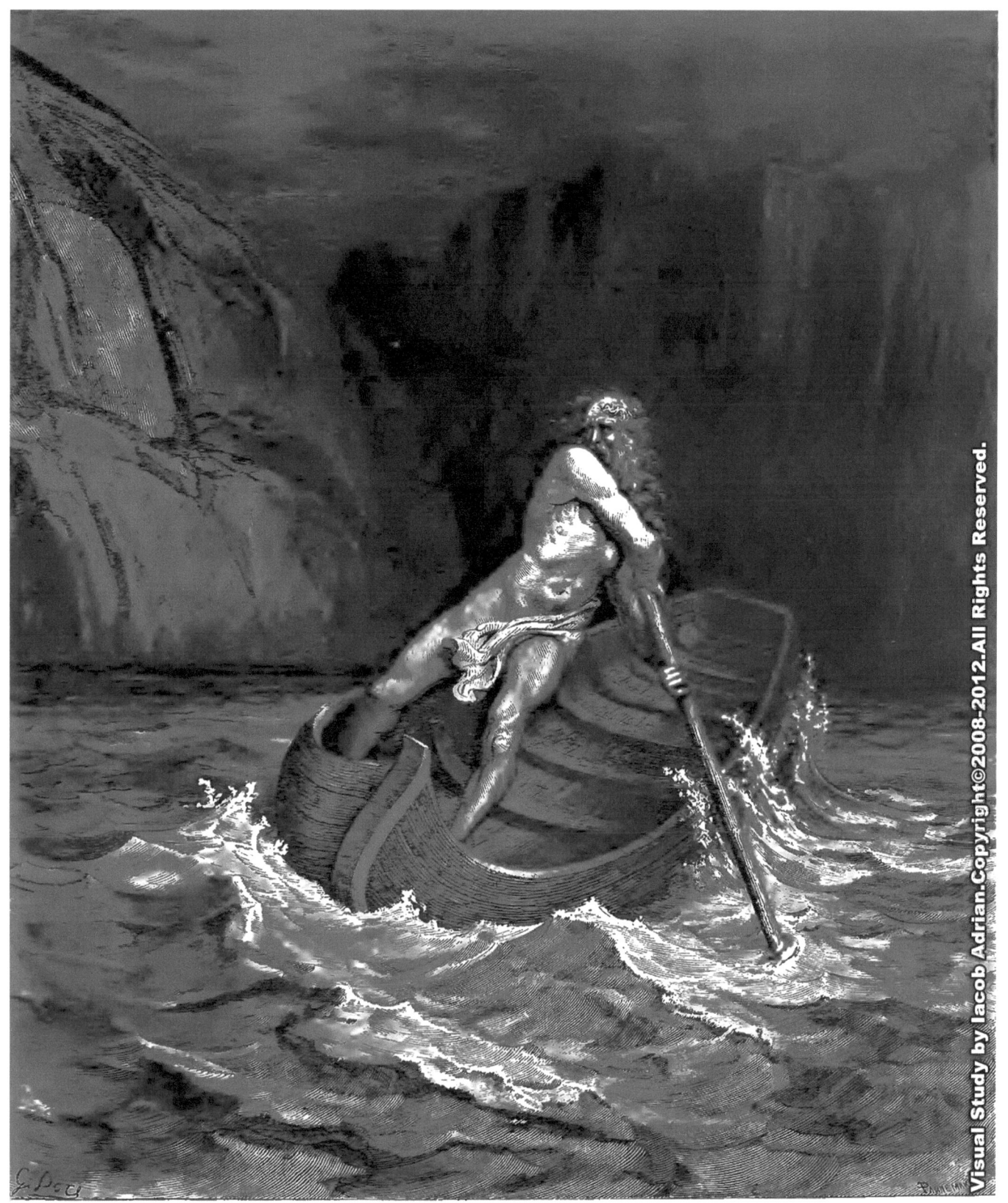

And, lo ! toward us in a bark
Comes on an old man, hoary white with eld,
Crying, " Woe to you, wicked spirits ! "

Canto III., lines 76-78.

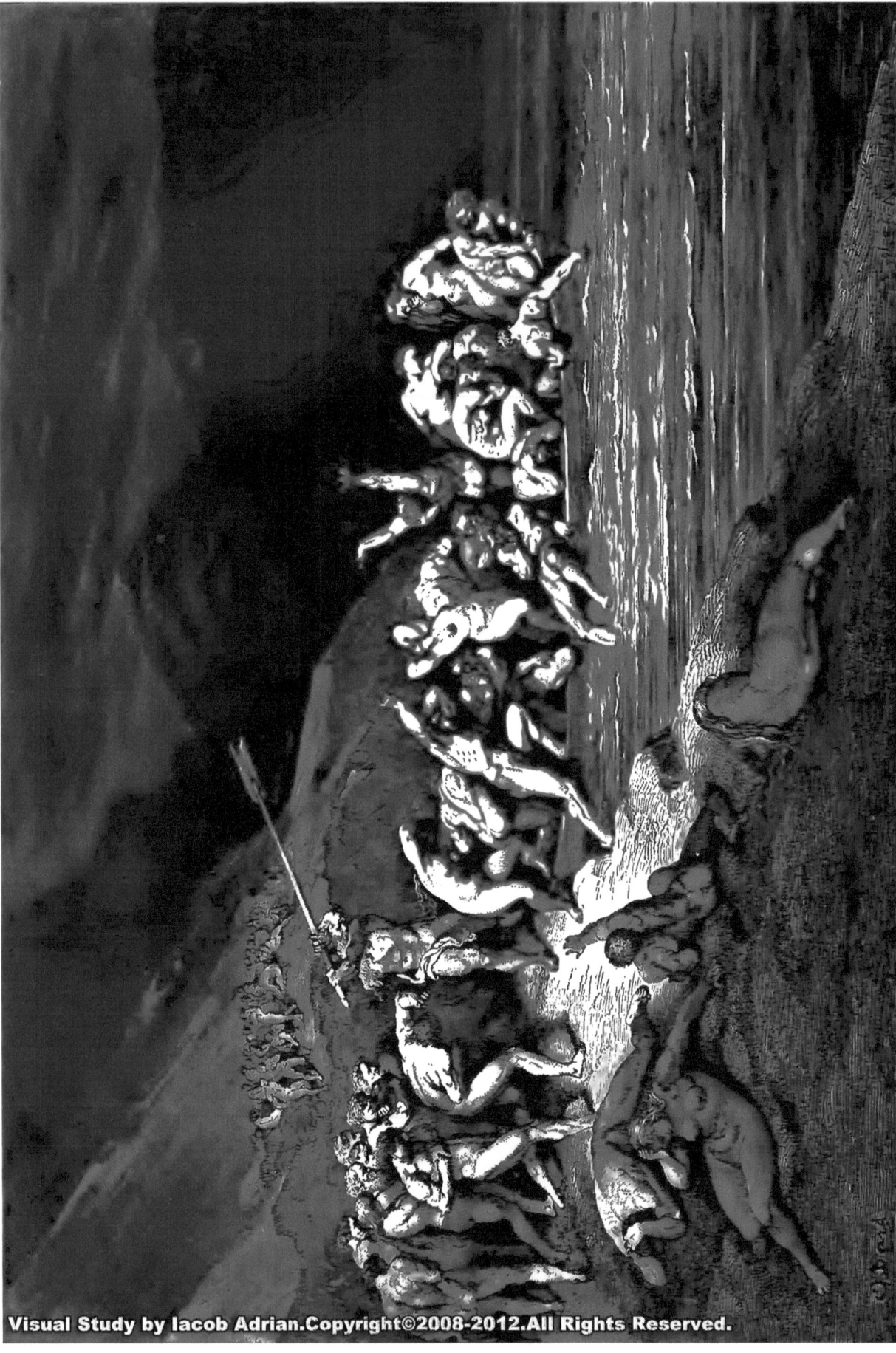

E'en in like manner Adam's evil brood
Cast themselves, one by one, down from the shore.
Canto III., lines 107, 108.

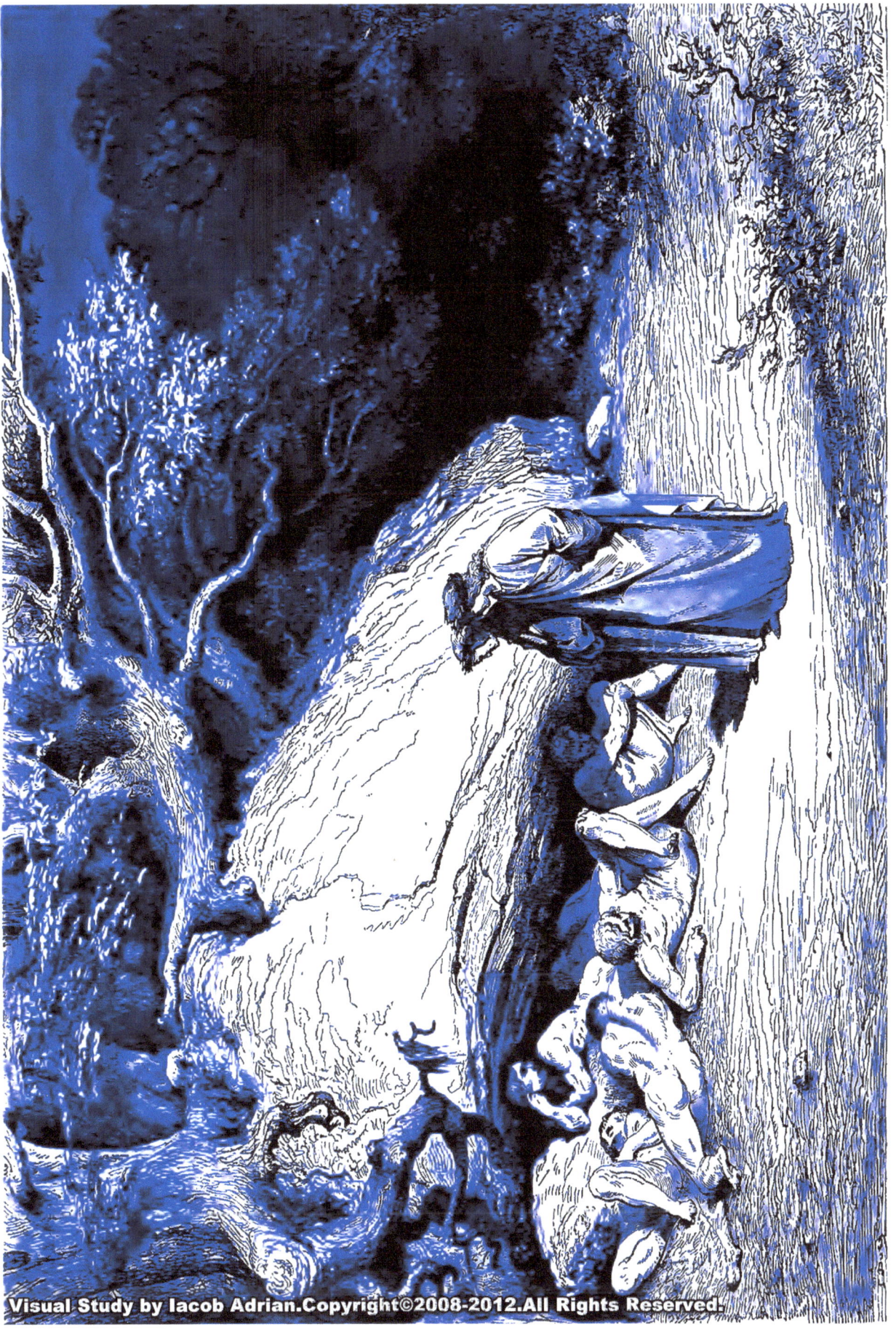

Only so far afflicted, that we live
Desiring without hope.   *Canto IV., lines 38, 39.*

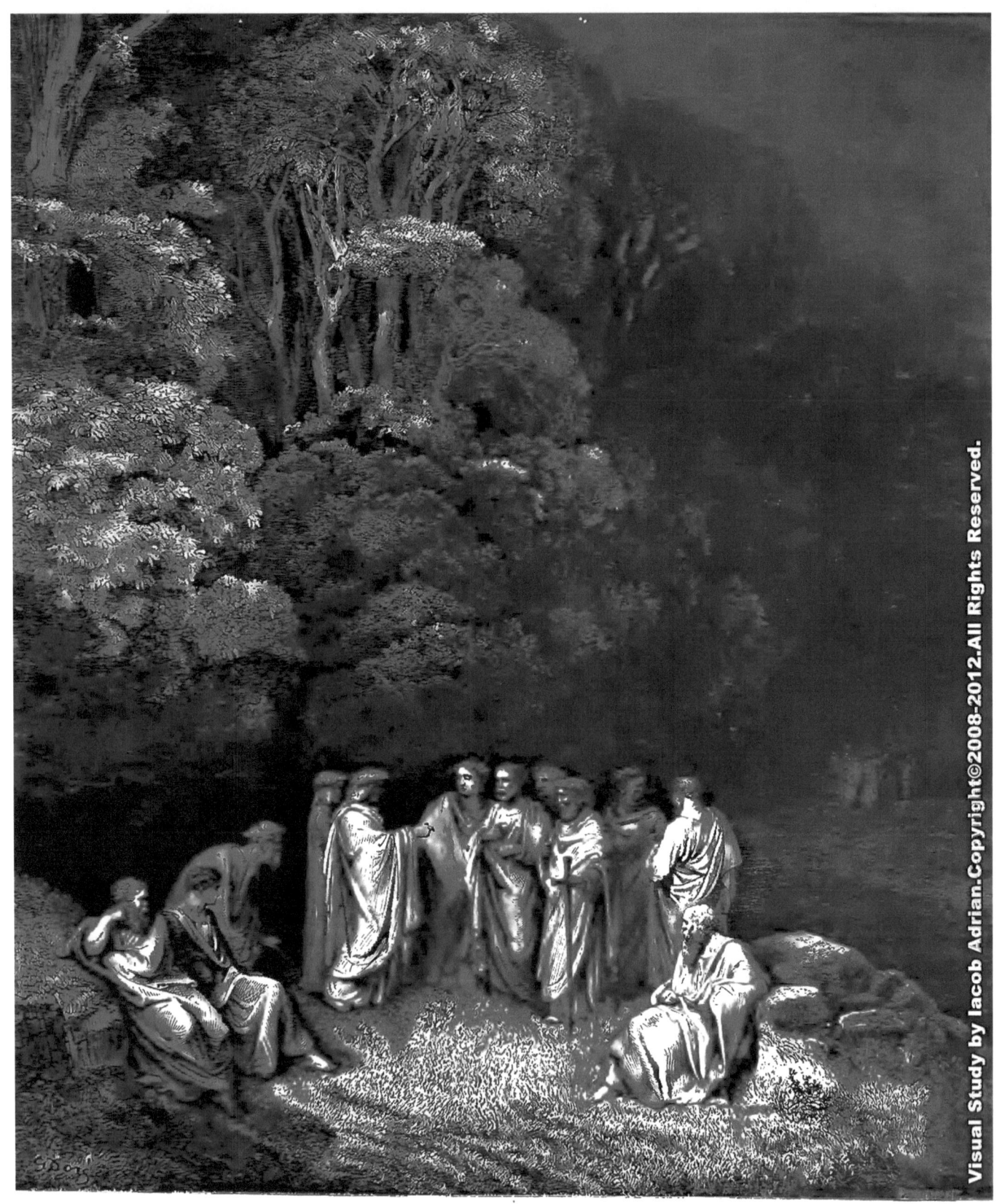

So I beheld united the bright school
Of him the monarch of sublimest song,
That o'er the others like an eagle soars.

Canto IV., lines 89-91.

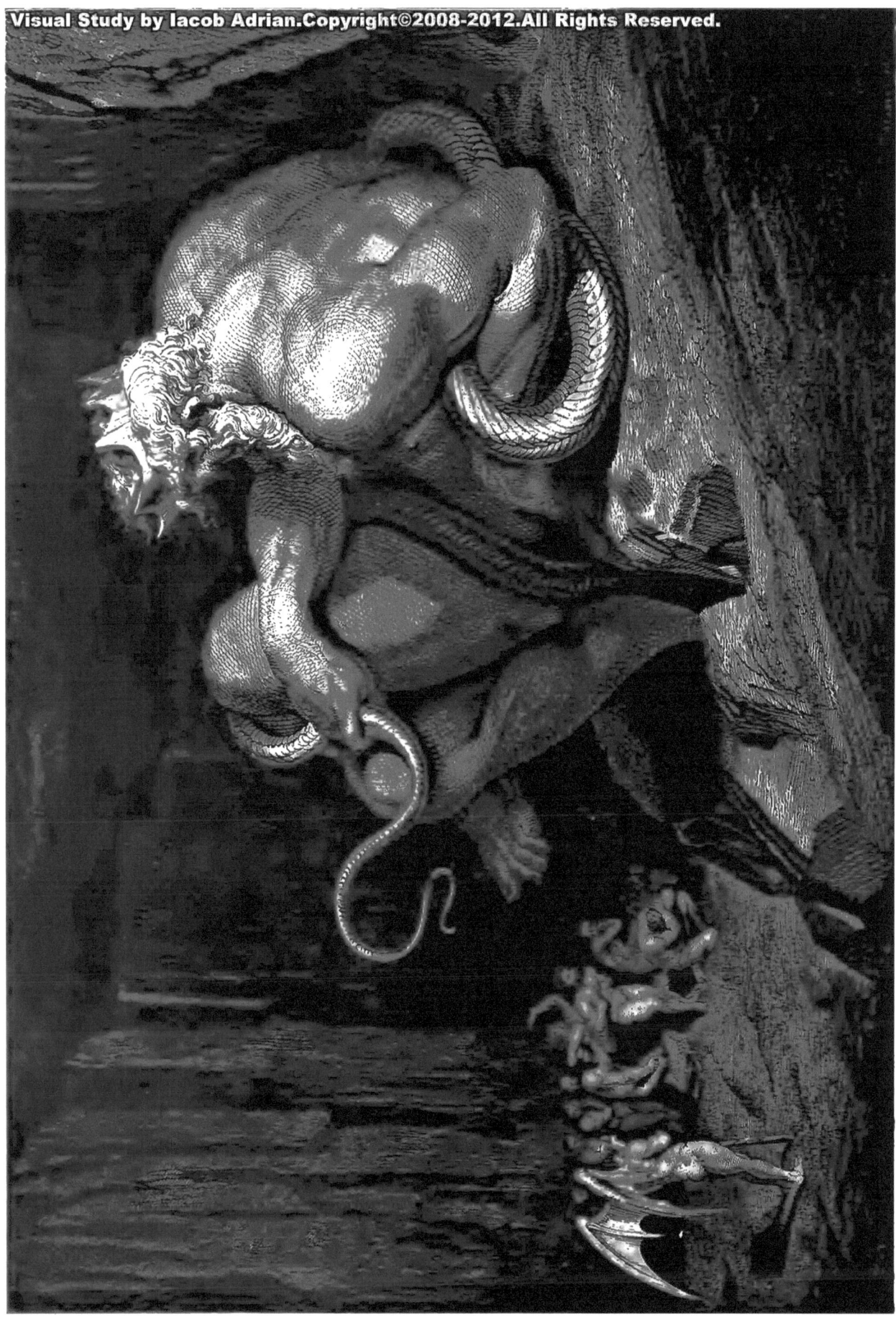

There Minos stands. *Canto V., line 4.*

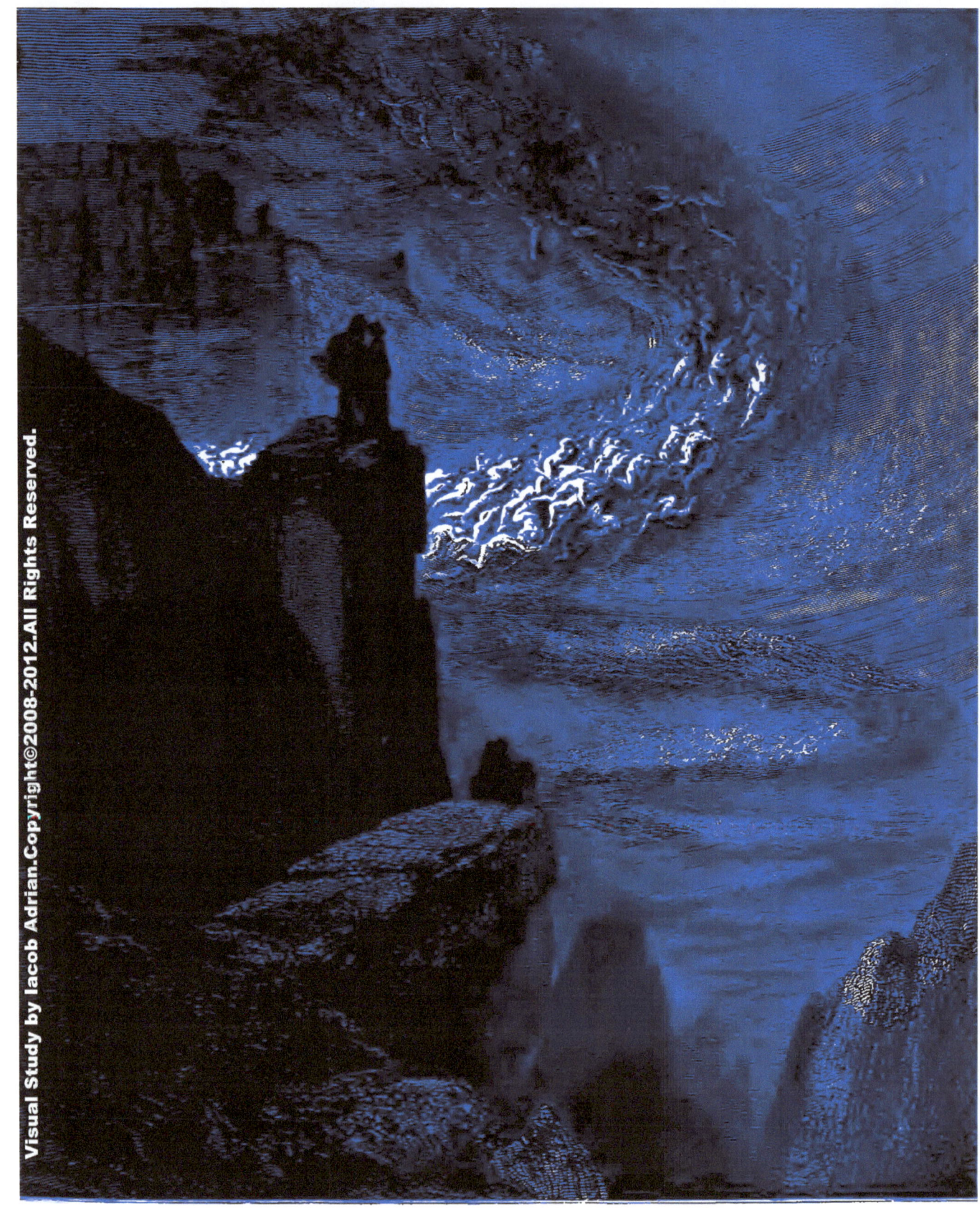

The stormy blast of hell
With restless fury drives the spirits on.

Canto V., *lines* 32, 33.

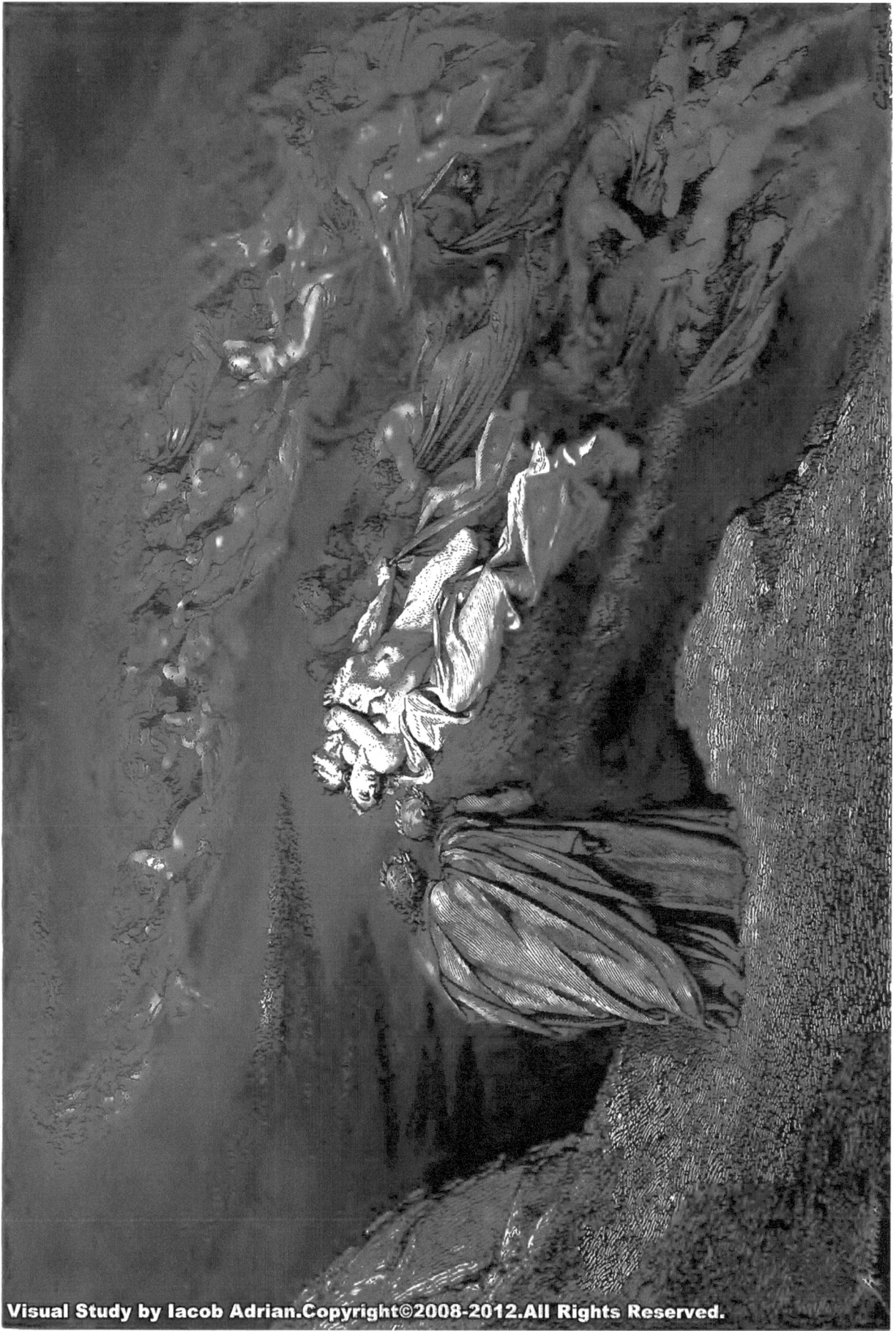

Love brought us to one death : Caïna waits
The soul who spilt our life.

Canto V., lines 105, 106.

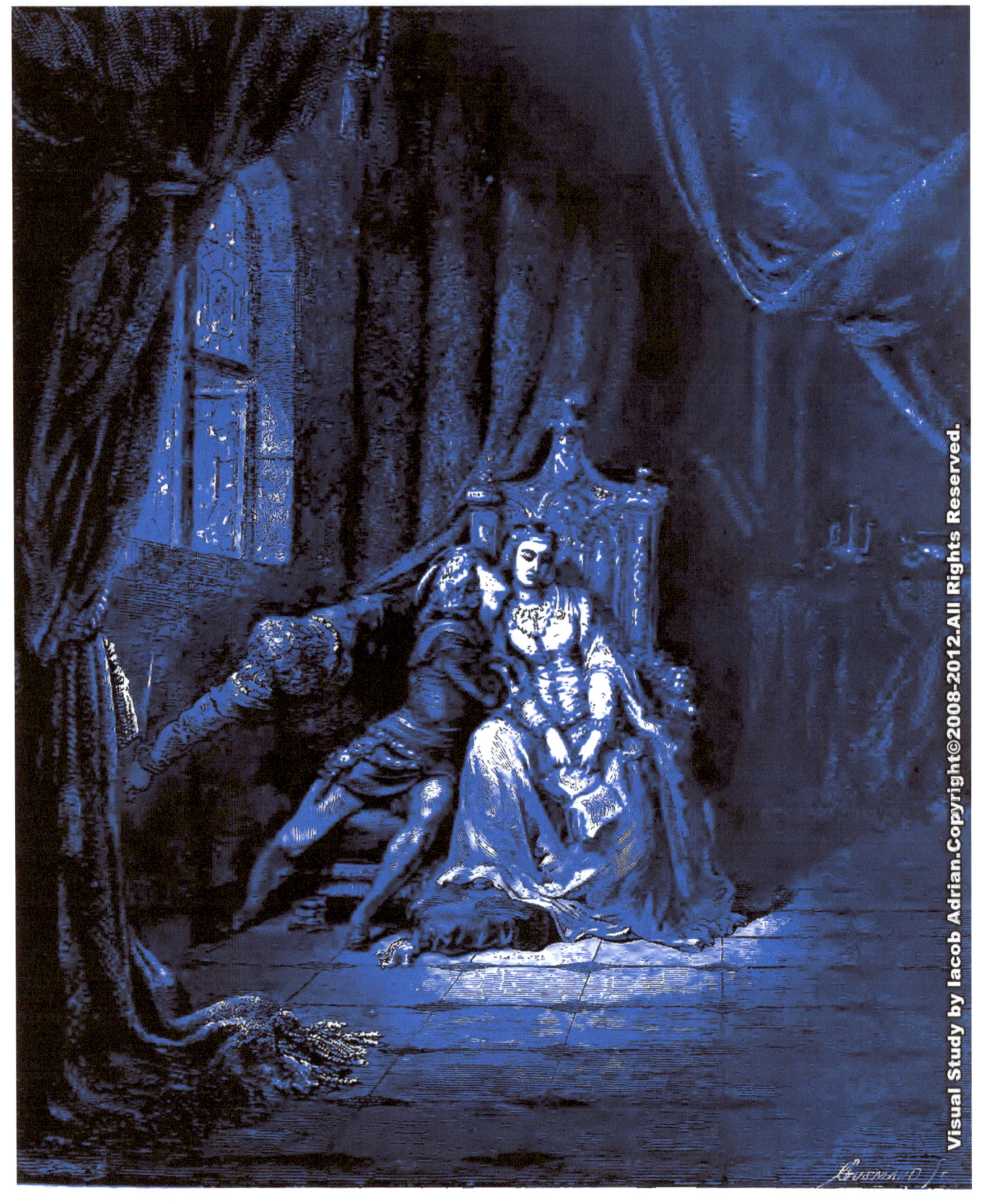

In its leaves that day

We read no more.

Canto V., lines 134, 135.

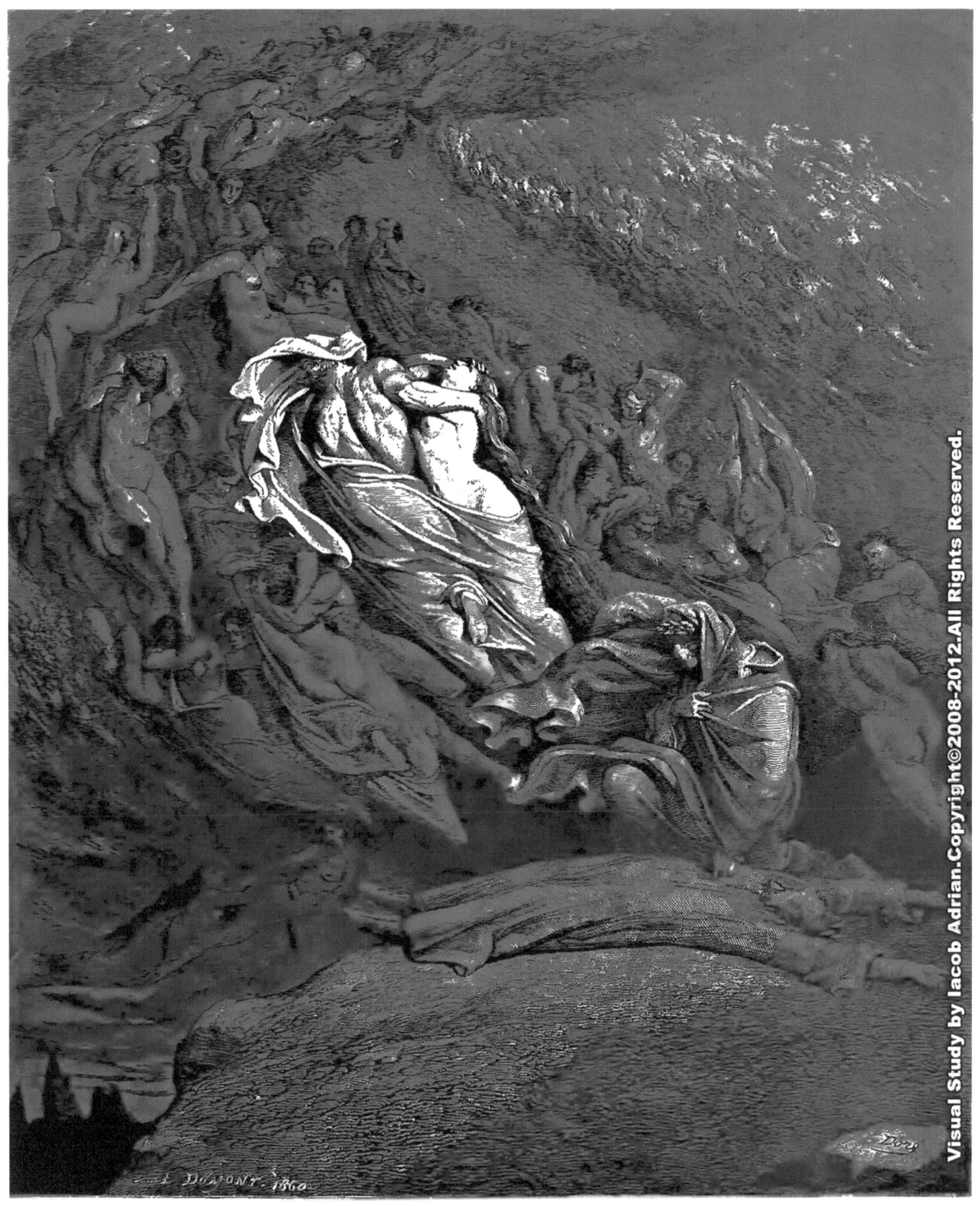

I, through compassion fainting, seem'd not far
From death, and like a corse fell to the ground.

Canto V., lines 137, 138.

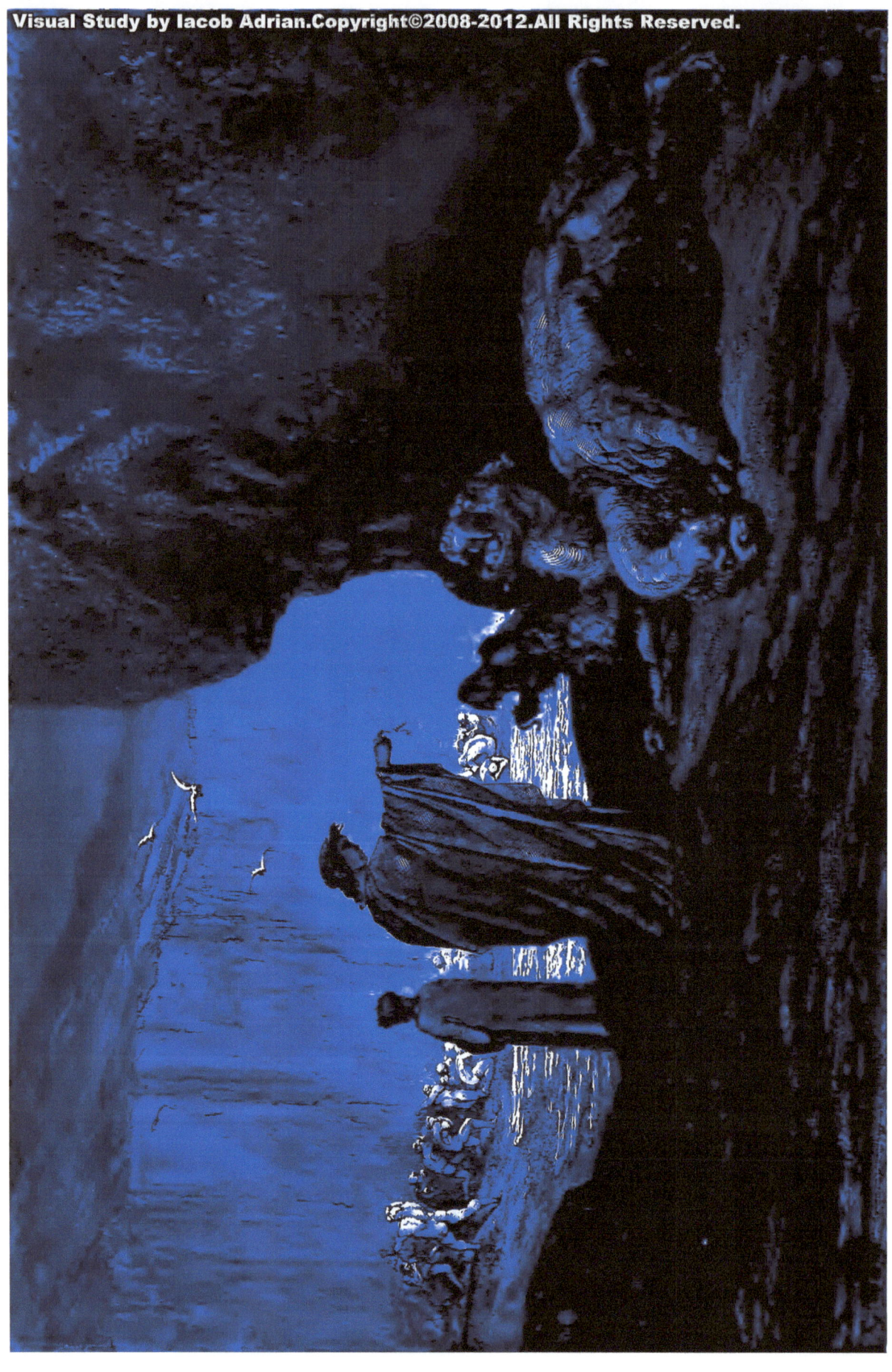

Then my guide, his palms
Expanding on the ground, thence fill'd with earth
Raised them, and cast it in his ravenous maw.
Canto VI., lines 24—26.

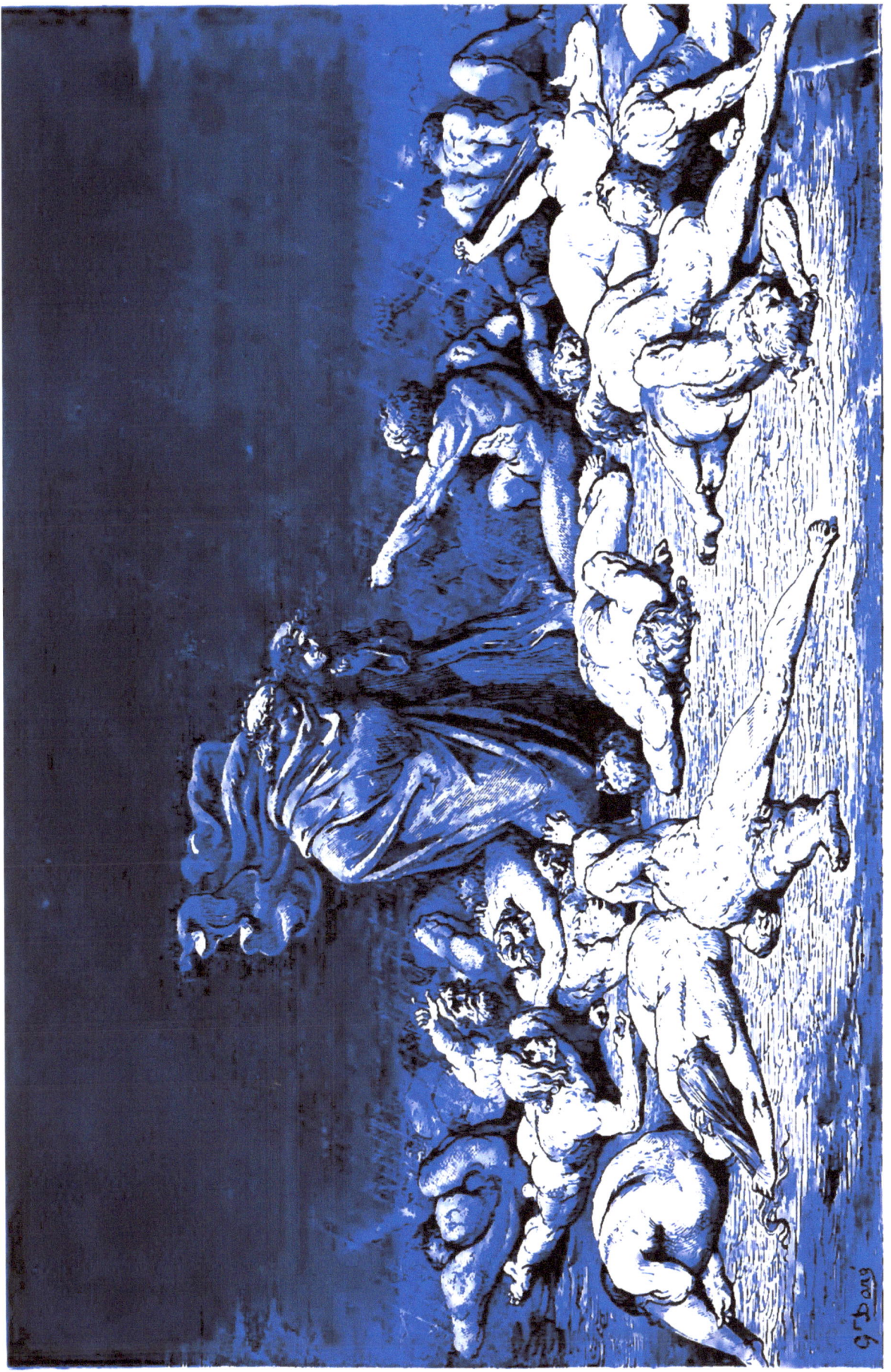

Thy city, heap'd with envy to the brim,
Aye, that the measure overflows its bounds,
Held me in brighter days. Ye citizens
Were wont to name me Ciacco.

Canto VI., lines 49—52.

Curst wolf! thy fury inward on thyself
Prey; and consume thee!

Canto VII. lines 8, 9.

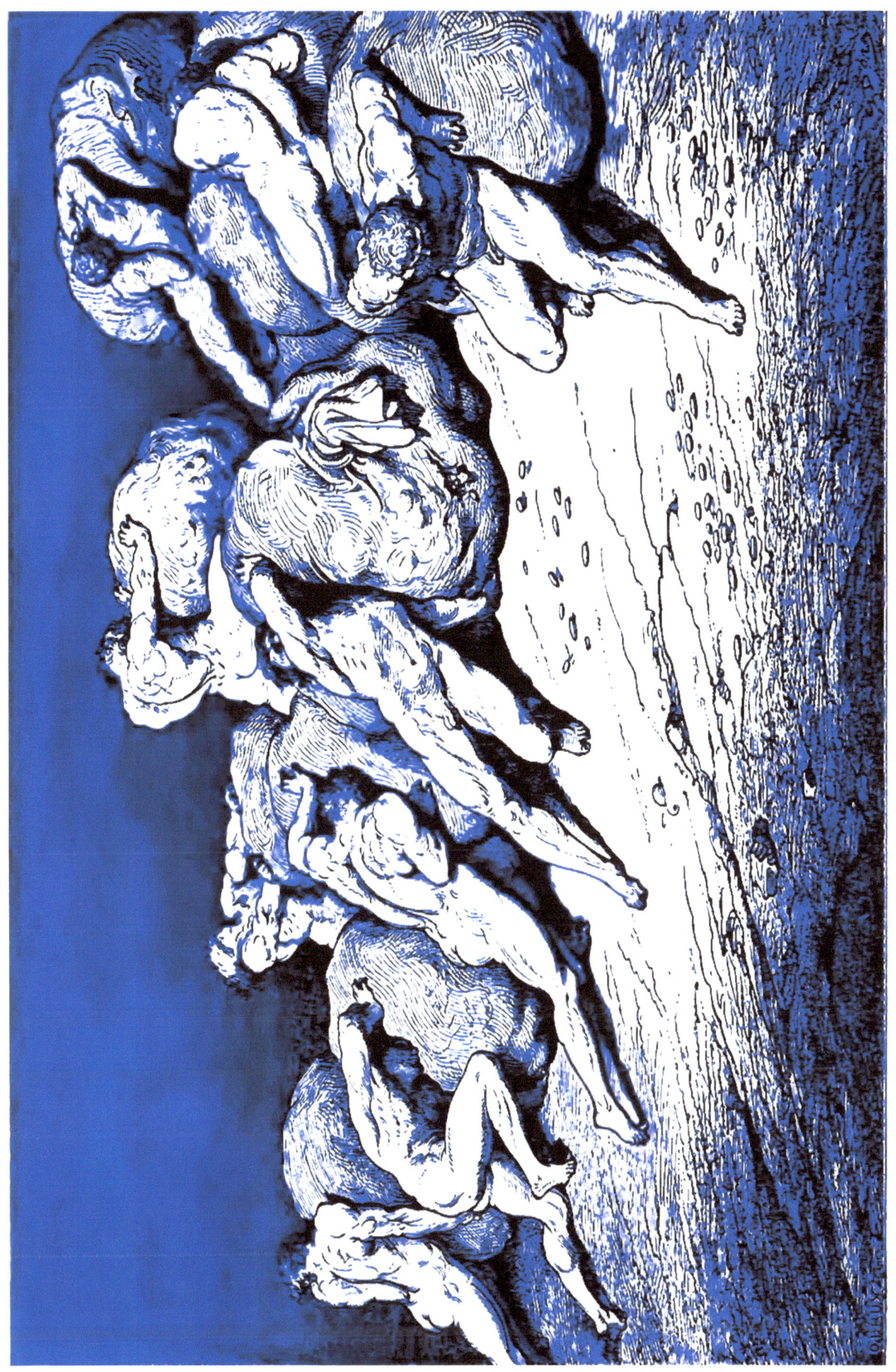

Not all the gold that is beneath the moon,
Or ever hath been, of these toil-worn souls
Might purchase rest for one.

Canto VII., lines 65—67.

Now seest thou, son !
The souls of those, whom anger overcame.
Canto VII., lines 118, 119.

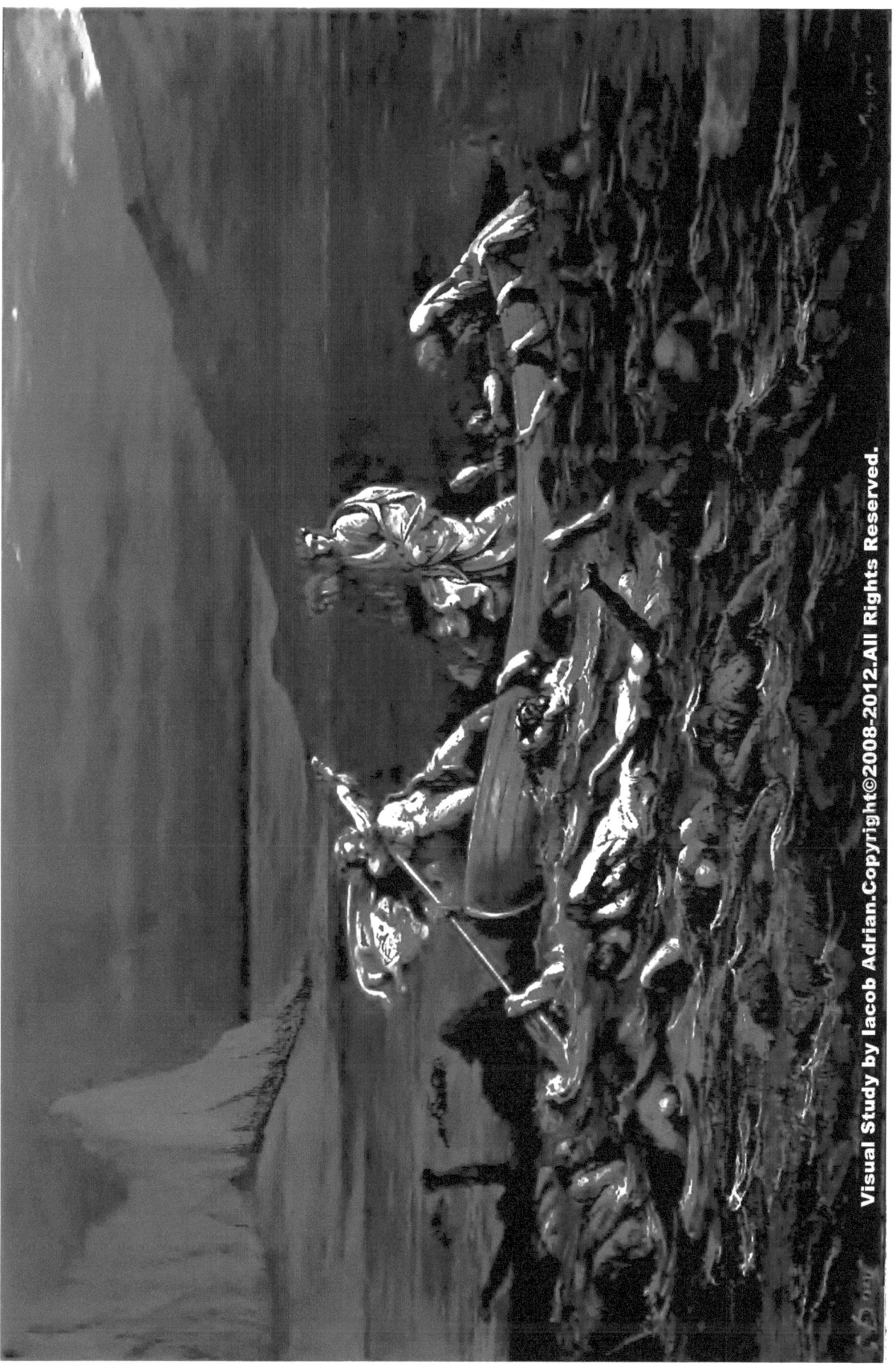

Soon as both embark'd,
Cutting the waves, goes on the ancient prow,
More deeply than with others it is wont.
Canto VIII., lines 27—29.

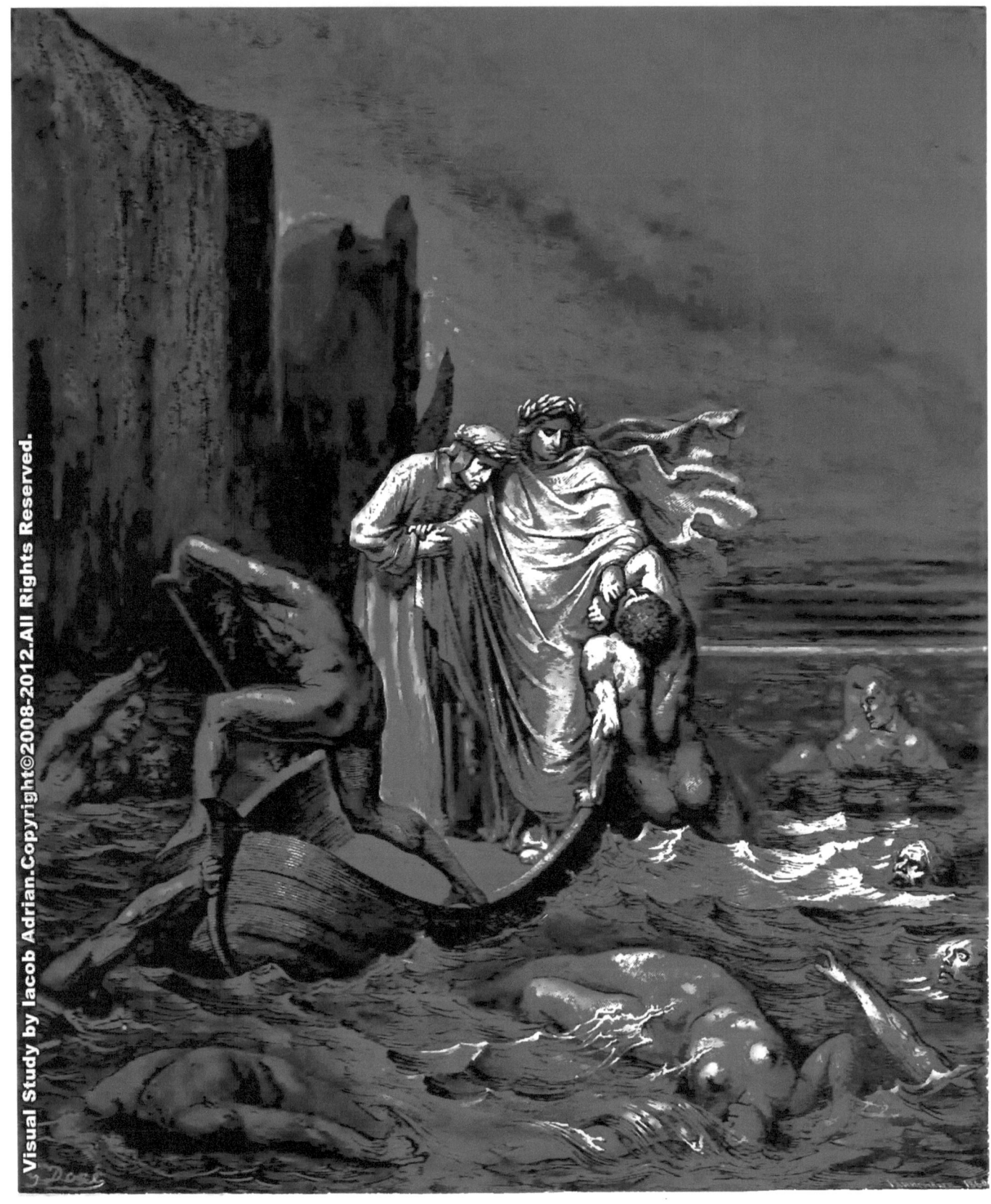

My teacher sage
Aware, thrusting him back: "Away! down there
To the other dogs!"

Canto VIII., lines 39-41.

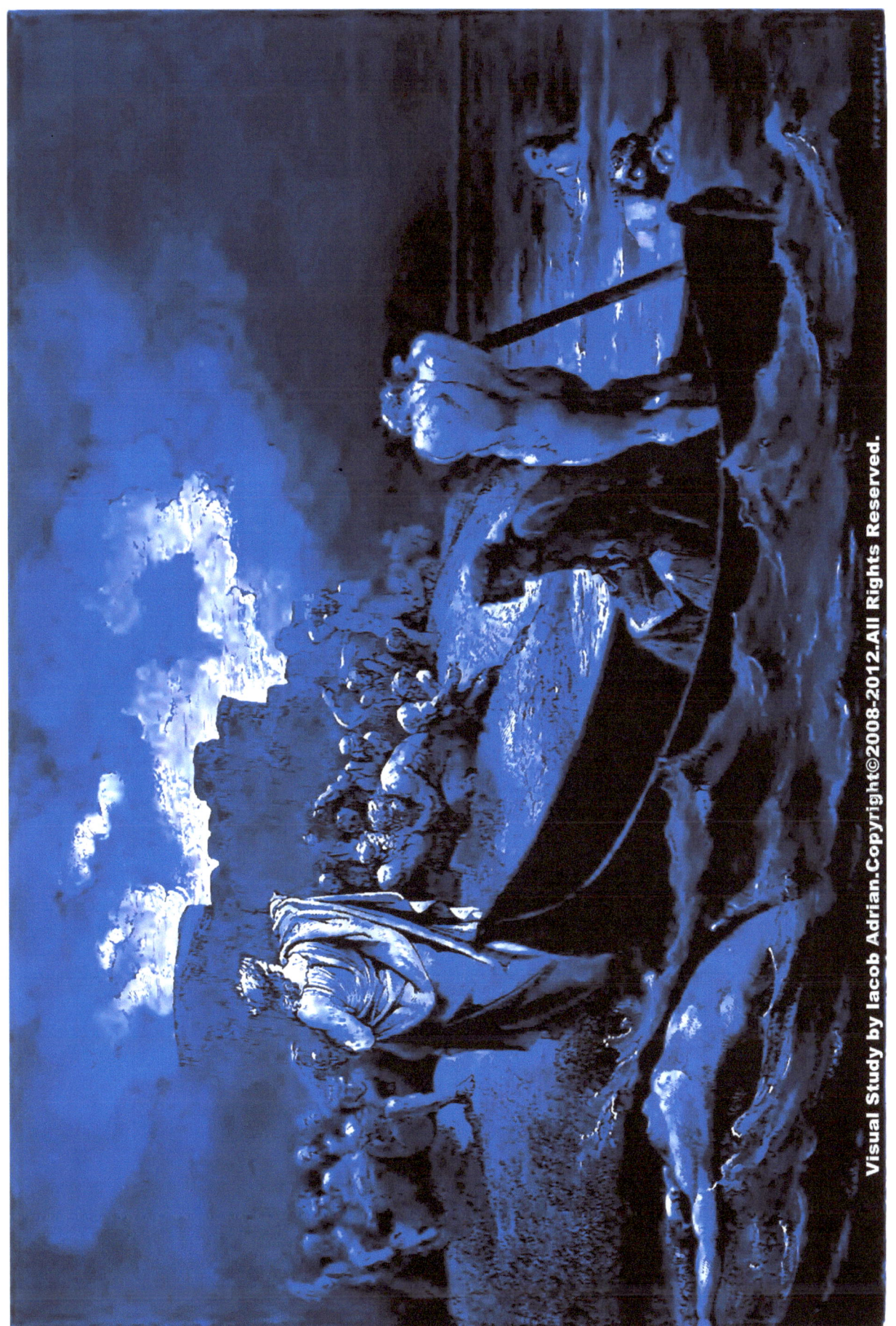

I could not hear what terms he offer'd them,
But they conferr'd not long.

Canto VIII., lines 110, 111.

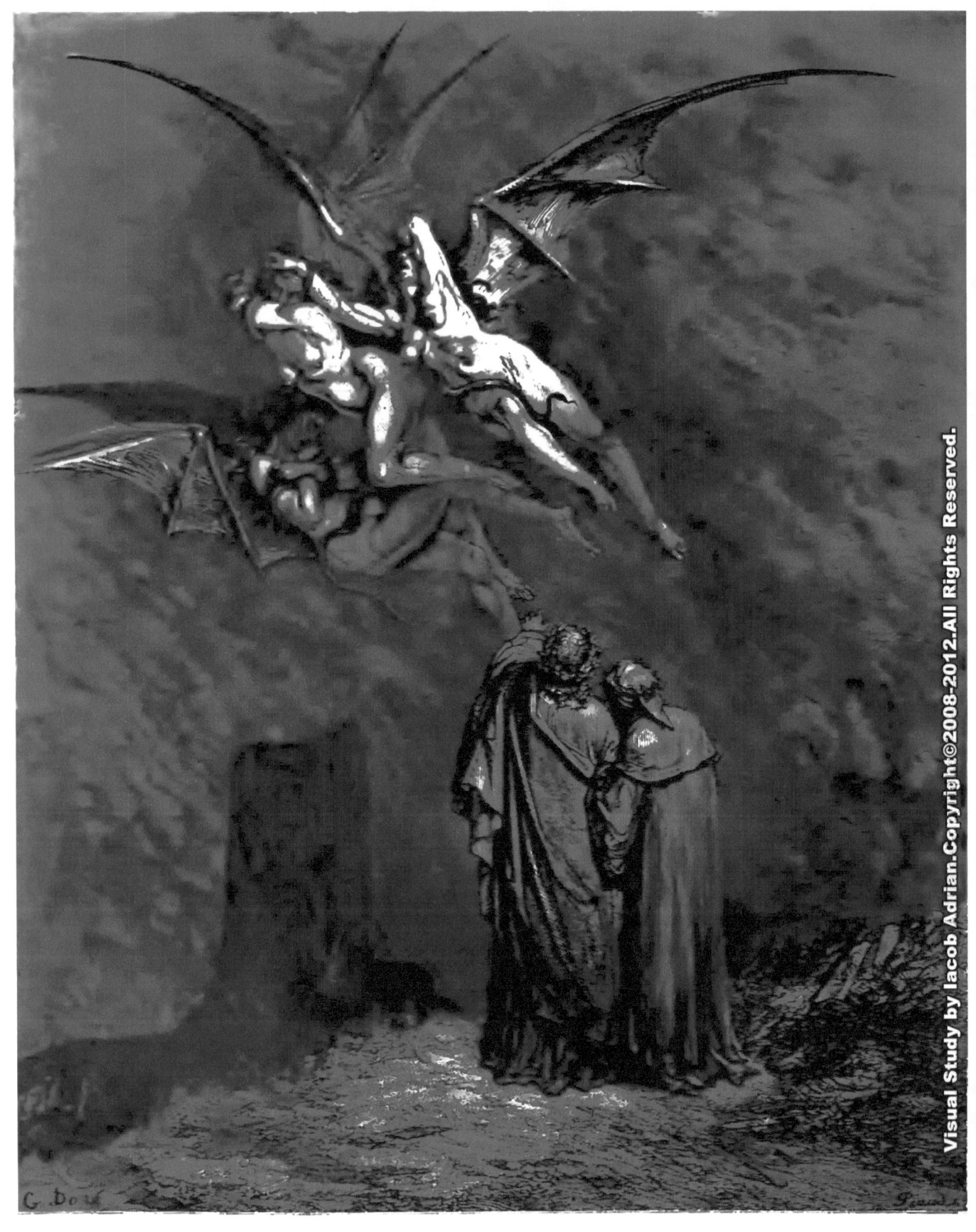

Mark thou each dire Erynnis.

Canto IX., line 46.

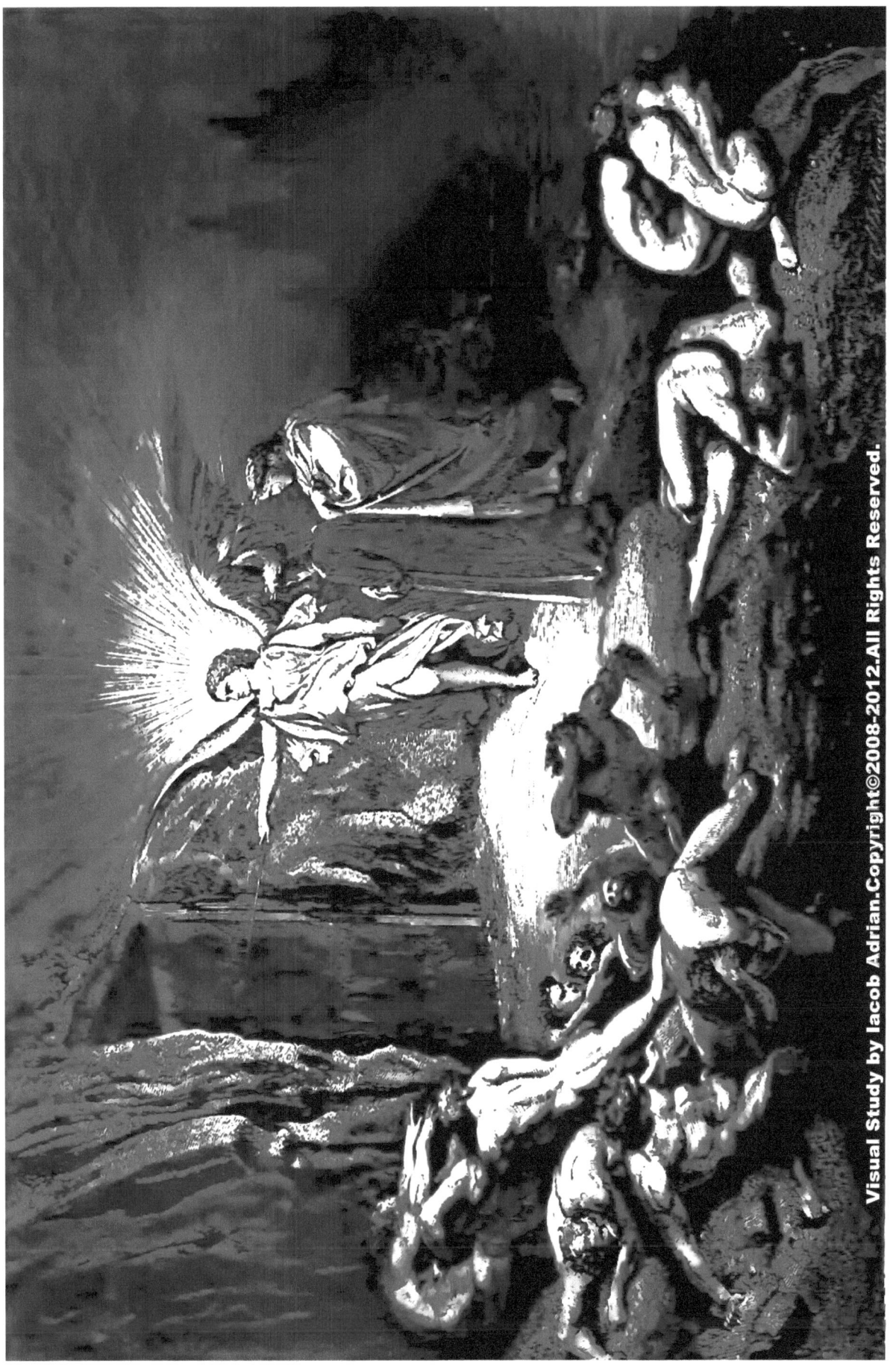

To the gate
He came, and with his wand touch'd it, whereat
Open without impediment it flew.

Canto IX., lines 87—89.

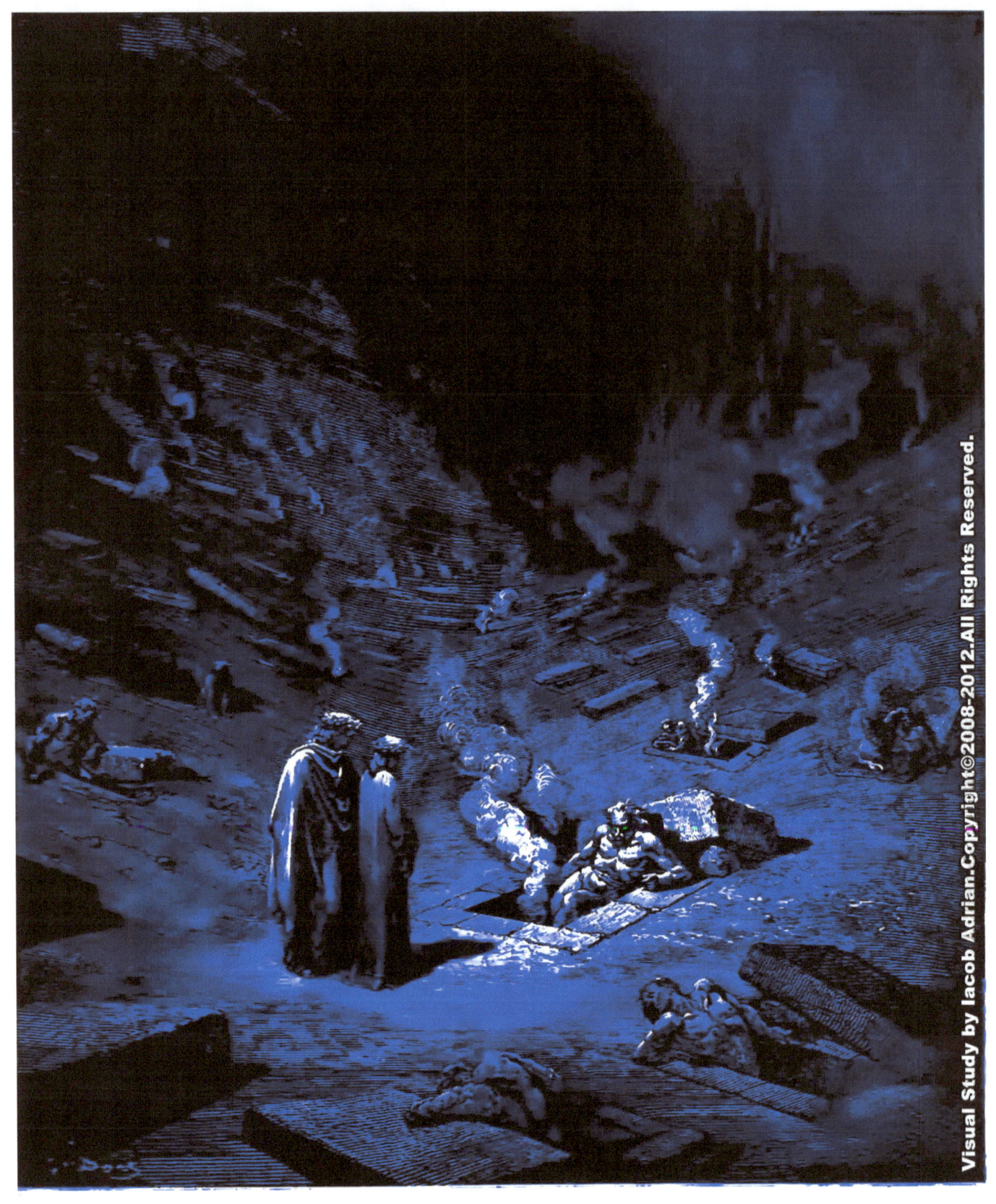

He answer thus return'd :
"The arch-heretics are here, accompanied
By every sect their followers."

Canto IX., lines 124-126.

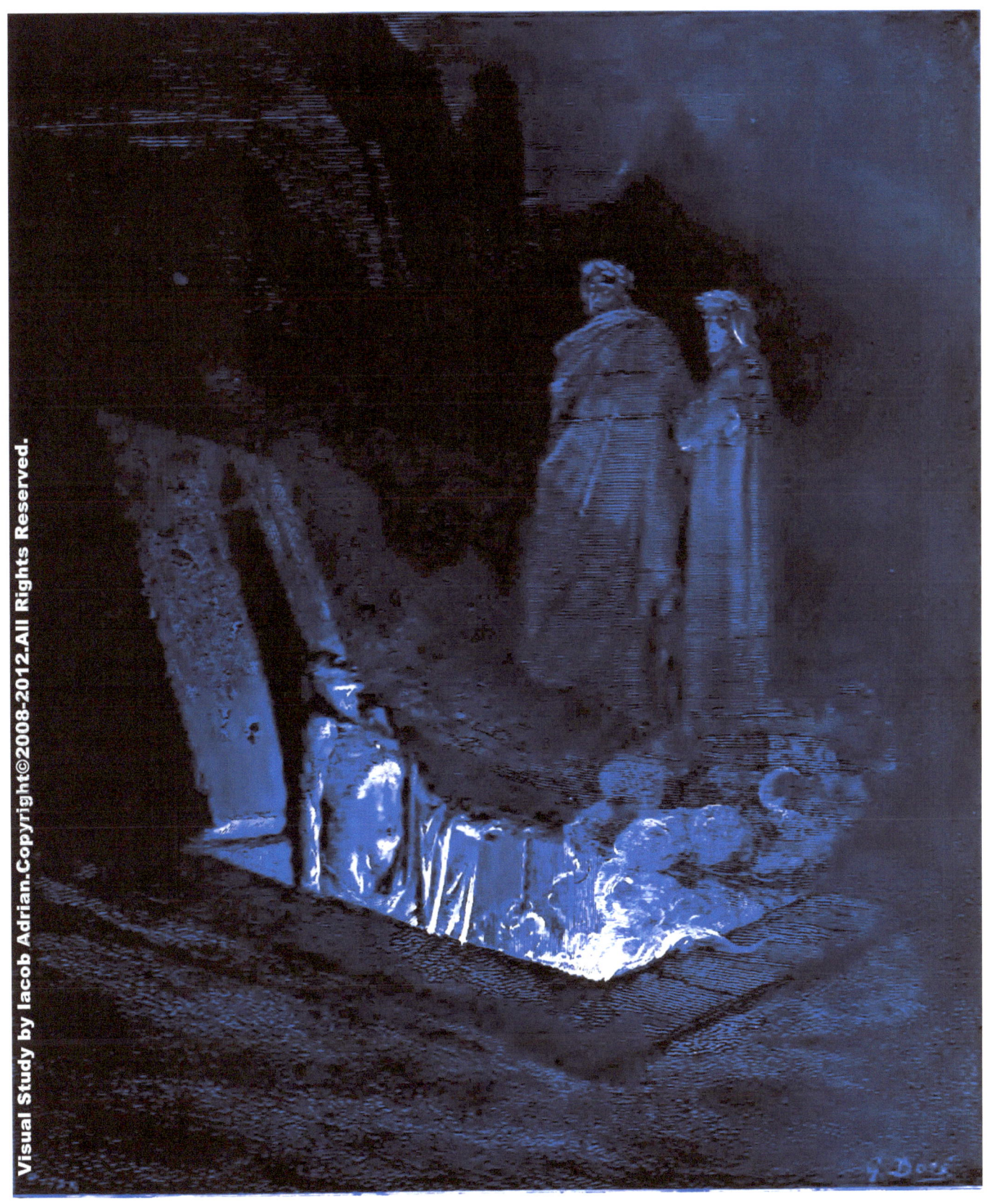

He, soon as there I stood at the tomb's foot,
Eyed me a space ; then in a disdainful mood
Address'd me : " Say what ancestors were thine."

Canto X , lines 40-42.

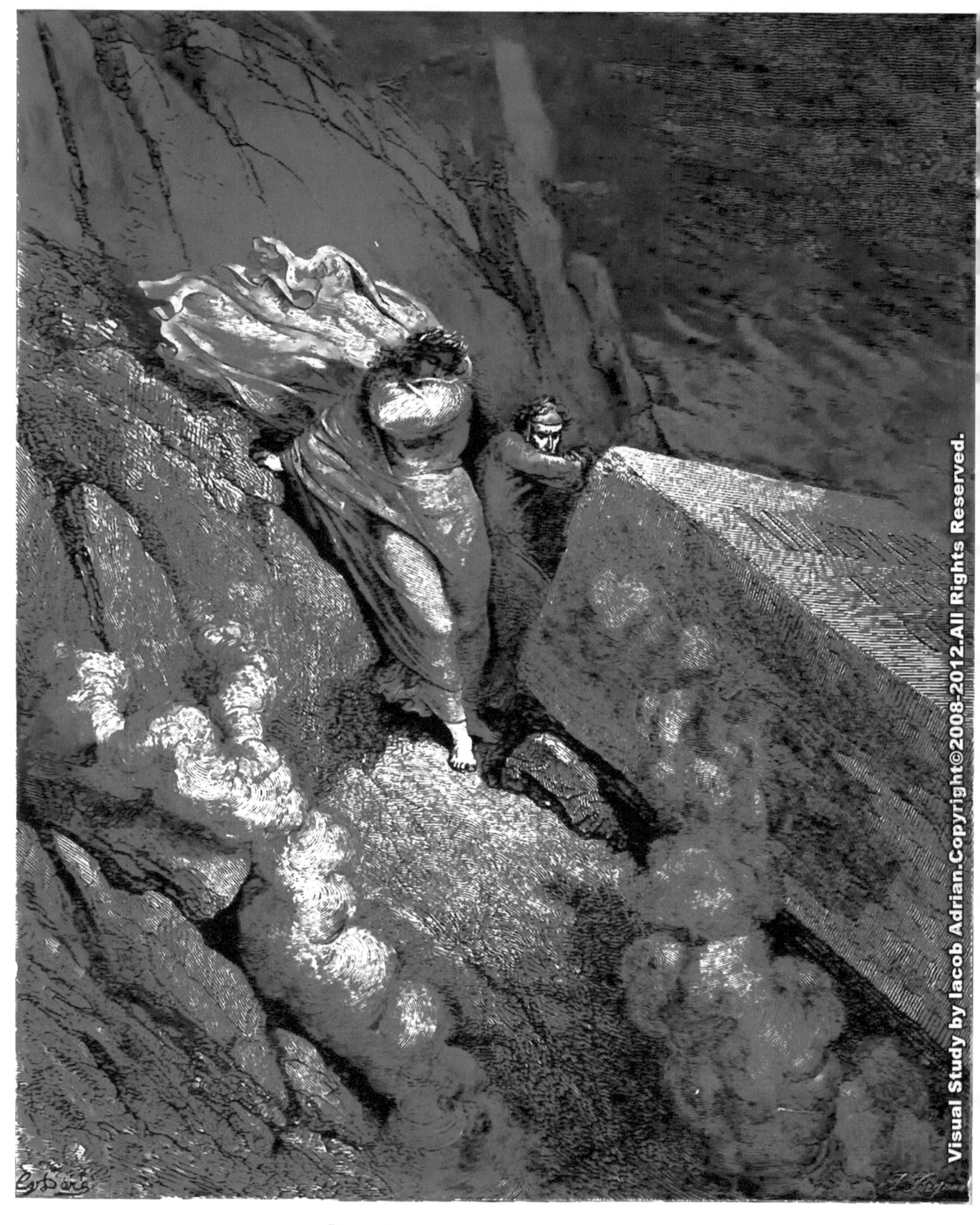

From the profound abyss, behind the lid
Of a great monument we stood retired.

Canto XI., lines 6, 7.

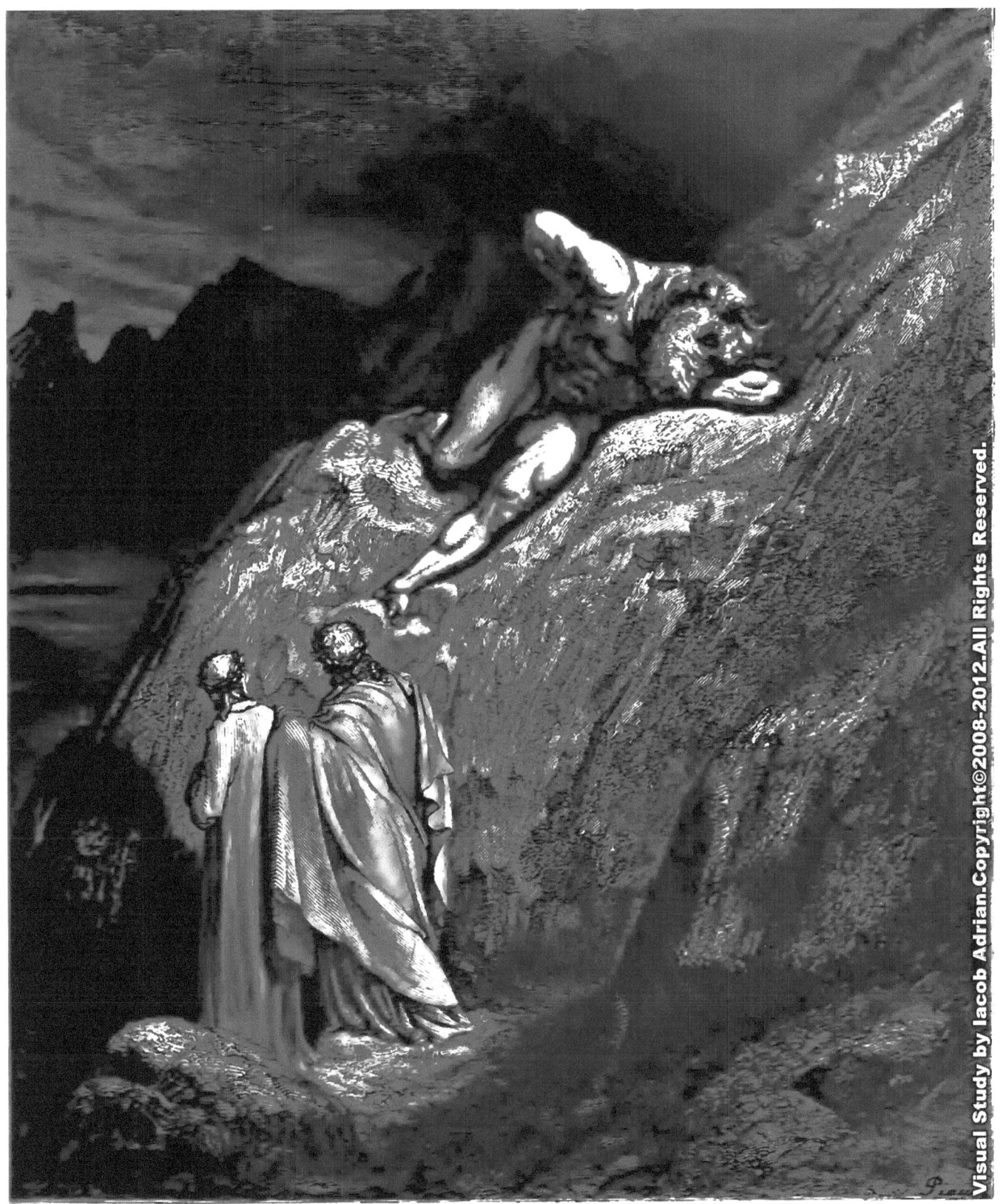

And there
At point of the disparted ridge lay stretch'd
The infamy of Crete, detested brood
Of the feign'd heifer.

Canto XII., *lines* 11-14.

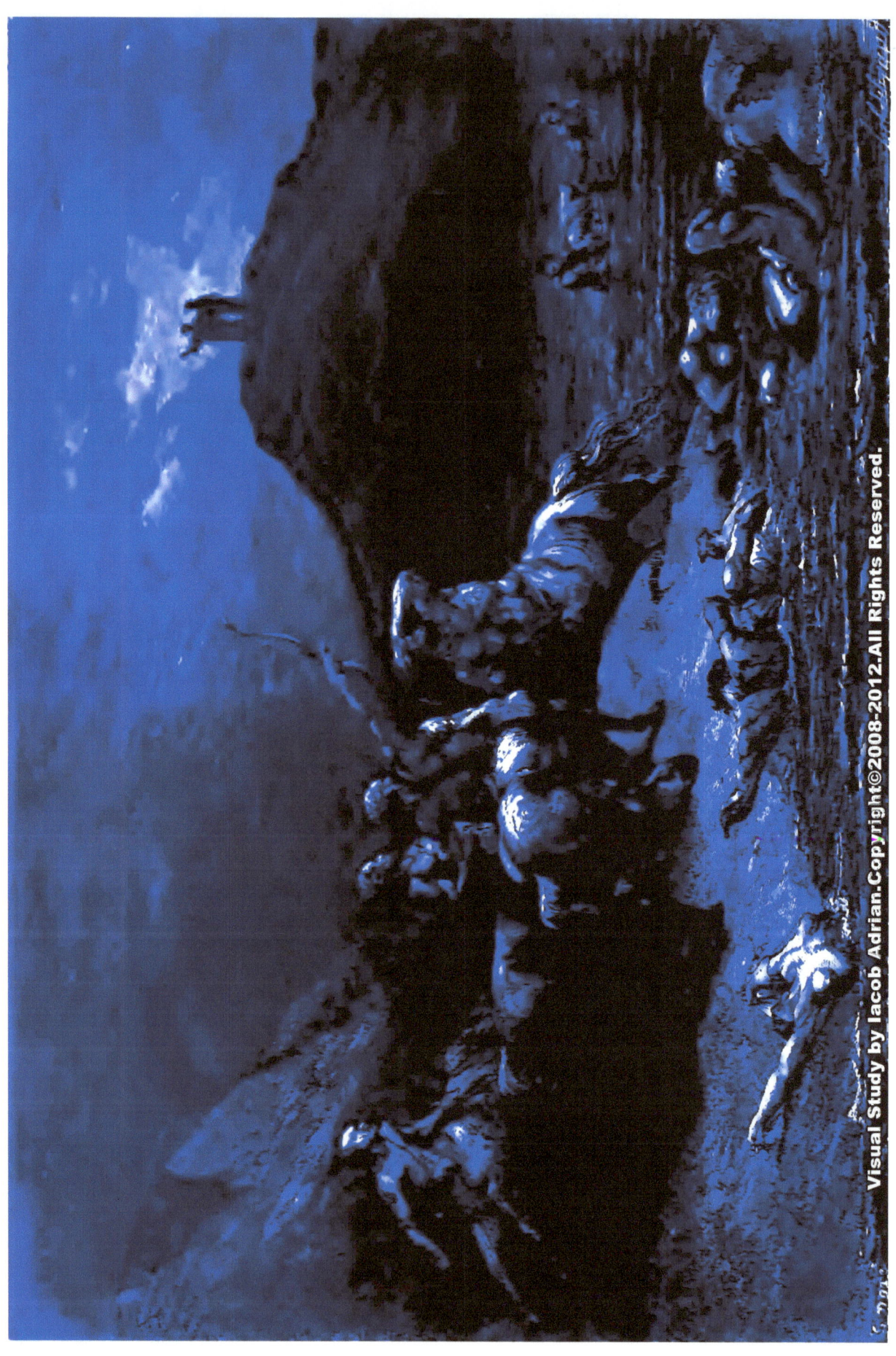

One cried from far : " Say, to what pain ye come
Condemn'd, who down this steep have journey'd."
Canto XII., lines 58, 59.

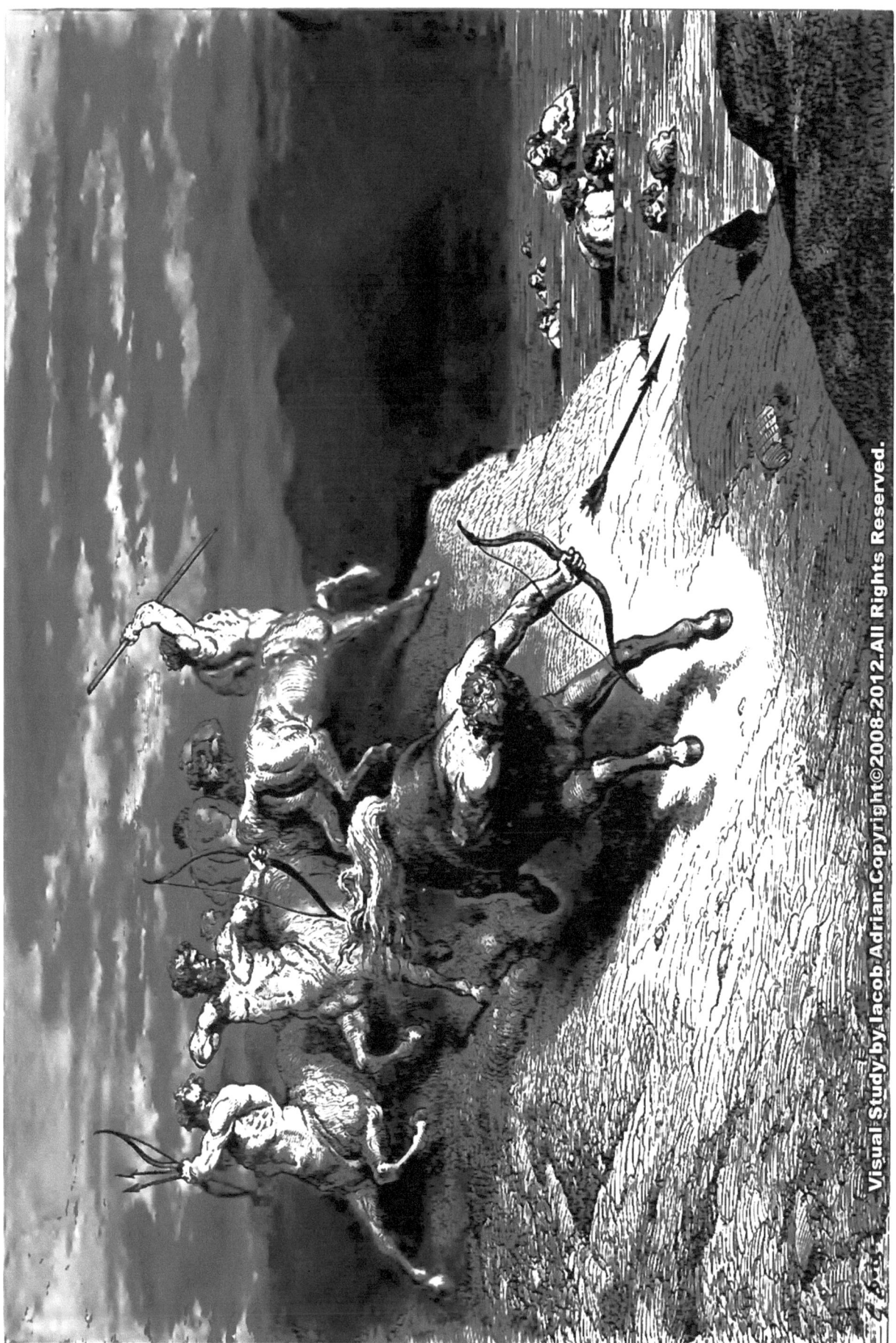

We to those beasts, that rapid strode along,
Drew near.

Canto XII , lines 73, 74

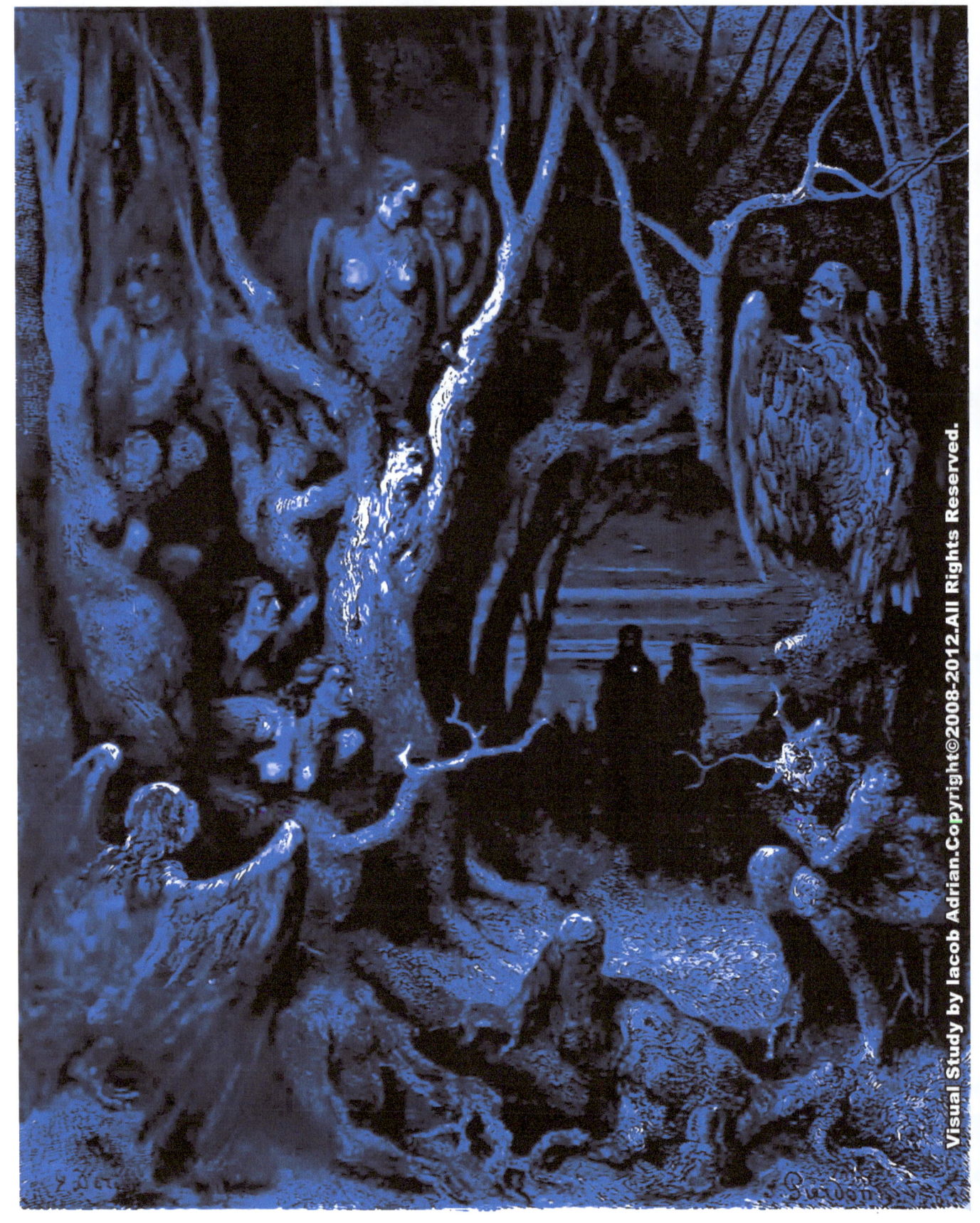

Here the brute Harpies make their nest.

Canto XIII., line **11.**

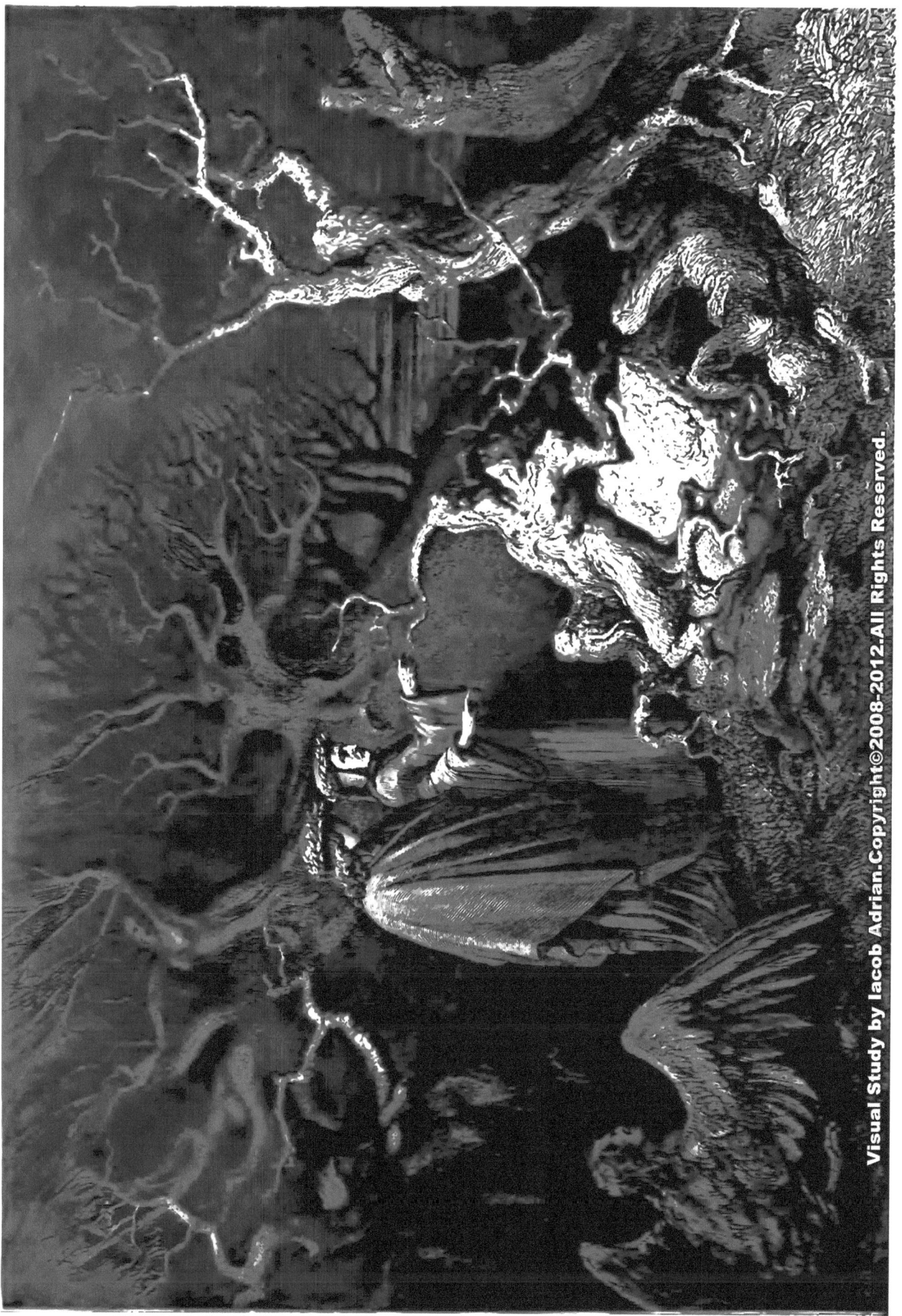

And straight the trunk exclaim'd, " Why pluck'st thou me?"

Canto XIII., line 34.

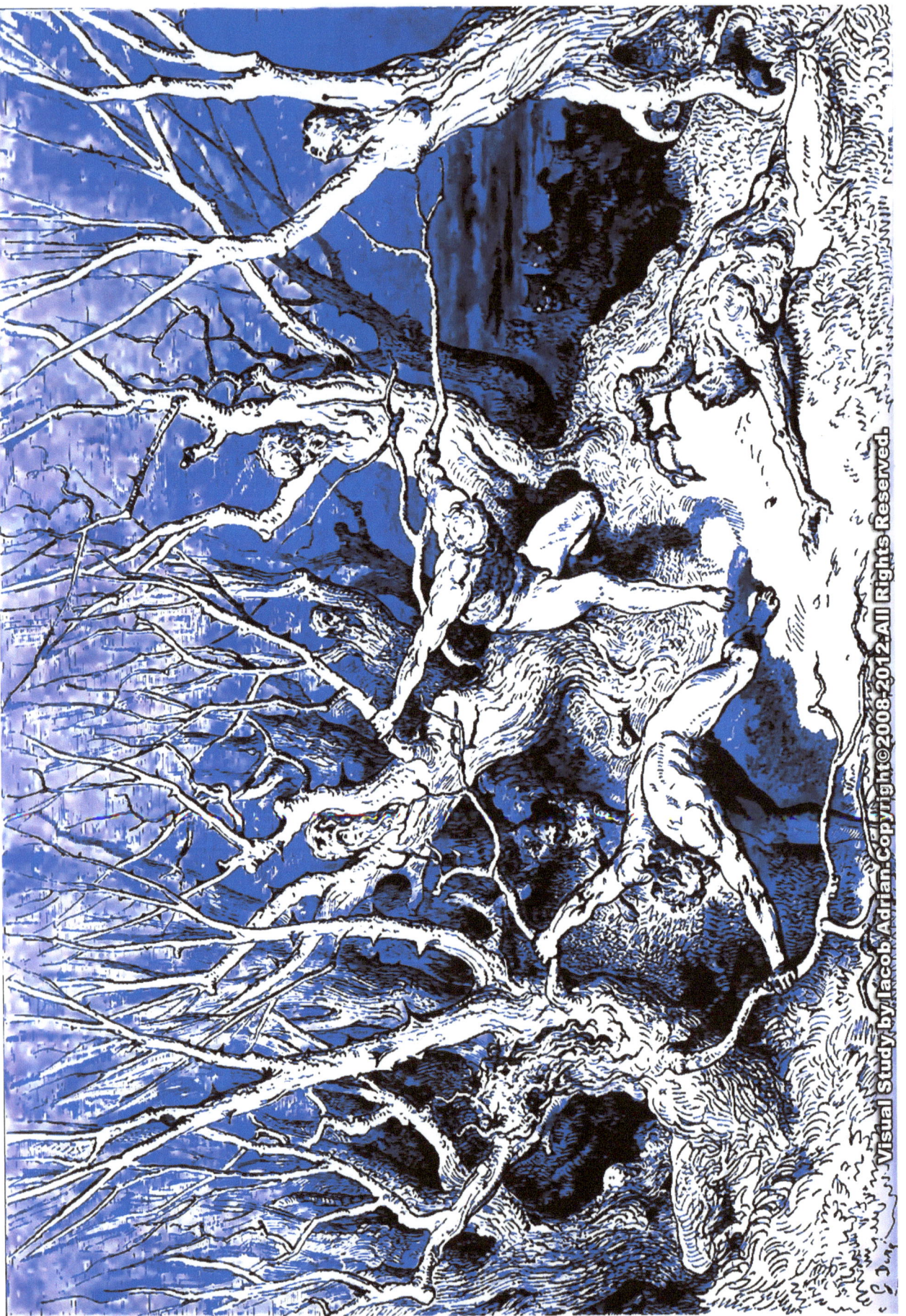

" Haste now," the foremost cried, " now haste thee, death !"
Canto XIII., line 120.

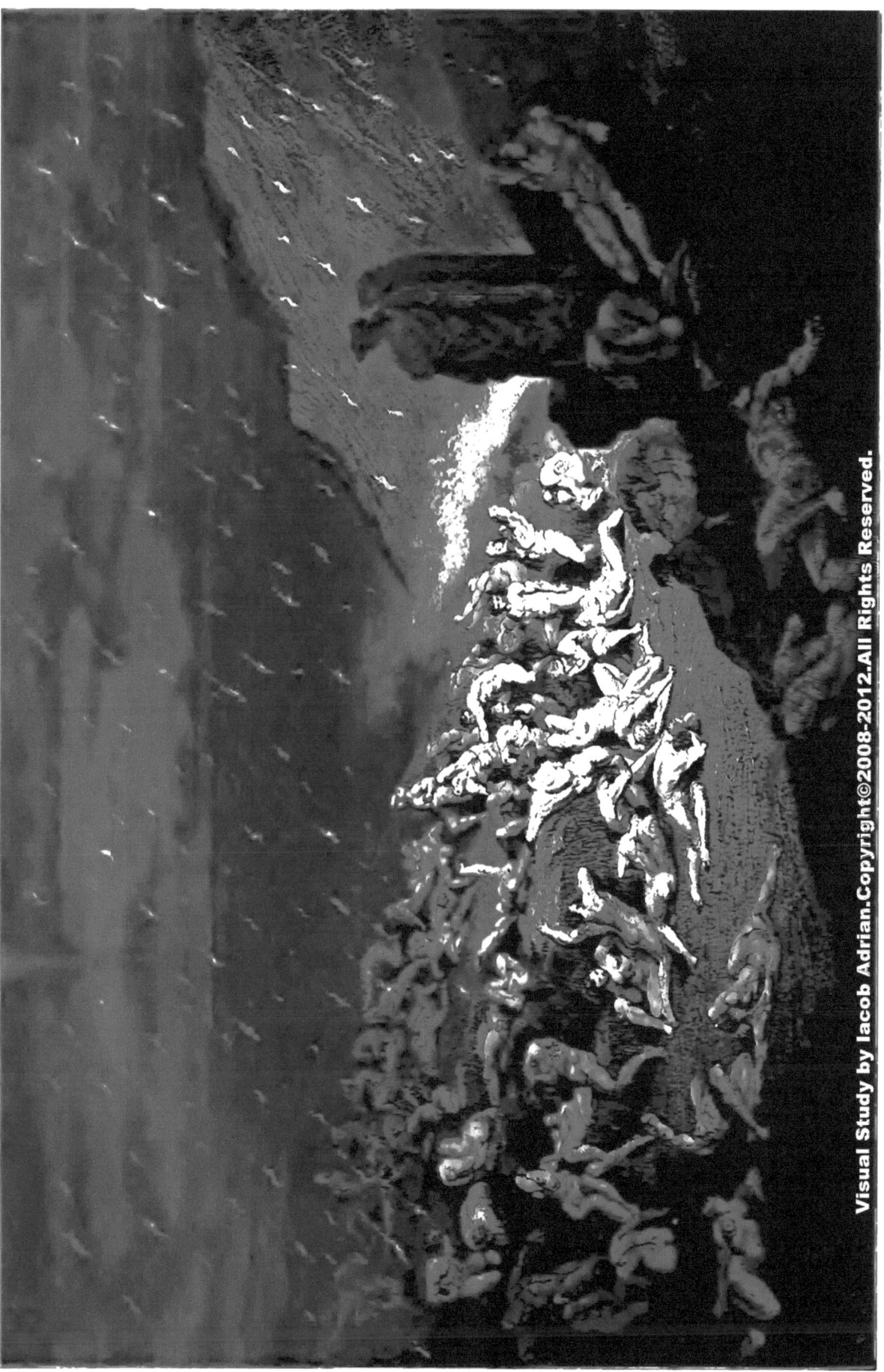

Unceasing was the play of wretched hands,
Now this, now that way glancing, to shake off
The heat, still falling fresh.

Canto XIV., lines 37—39.

Bibliographic sources :

Dante's Inferno ([1866])

Author:
Dante Alighieri, 1265-1321;
Cary, Henry Francis, 1772-1844;
Doré, Gustave, 1832-1883

Publisher: New York : Cassell, Petter, Galpin & Co.

This documentary study use, combined in various proportions,
elements from the following categories, forms and subsets :
- fair use
- documentary
- documentary photography
- feature
- journalism
- arts journalism
- visual journalism
- photojournalism
- celebrity photography
in order to :
- employ material as the object of cultural critique ,
- quote to illustrate an argument or point ,
- use material in historical sequence,
providing independent opinion,
using photos, press articles, advertisements,
opinions of fans etc. ...

www.ingramcontent.com/pod-product-compliance
Lightning Source LLC
Chambersburg PA
CBHW051104180526
45172CB00002B/775